Contents

Rise & Shine

Aunt Marilyn's Cinnamon French Toast Casserole

1 large loaf French bread, cut into 1½-inch slices
3½ cups milk
9 eggs
1½ cups sugar, divided
1 tablespoon vanilla
½ teaspoon salt
6 to 8 medium baking apples, such as McIntosh or Cortland, peeled and sliced
1 teaspoon ground cinnamon
½ teaspoon ground nutmeg
Powdered sugar (optional)

1. Place bread slices in greased 13×9-inch baking dish or casserole.

2. Whisk milk, eggs, 1 cup sugar, vanilla and salt in large bowl until well blended. Pour half of mixture over bread. Layer apple slices over bread. Pour remaining half of egg mixture over apples.

3. Combine remaining ½ cup sugar, cinnamon and nutmeg in small bowl; sprinkle over casserole. Cover and refrigerate overnight.

4. Preheat oven to 350°F. Bake, uncovered, 1 hour or until egg mixture is set. Sprinkle with powdered sugar. *Makes 6 to 8 servings*

Delicious Ham & Cheese Puff Pie

2 cups (about 1 pound) diced cooked ham

1 package (10 ounces) frozen chopped spinach, thawed and
   squeezed dry

½ cup diced red bell pepper

4 green onions, sliced

3 eggs

¾ cup all-purpose flour

¾ cup (3 ounces) shredded Swiss cheese

¾ cup milk

1 tablespoon mustard

1 teaspoon grated lemon peel

1 teaspoon dried dill weed

½ teaspoon garlic salt

½ teaspoon black pepper

Fresh dill sprigs and lemon slices (optional)

1. Preheat oven to 425°F. Grease round 2-quart casserole.

2. Combine ham, spinach, bell pepper and green onions in prepared casserole. Beat eggs in medium bowl. Stir in flour, cheese, milk, mustard, lemon peel, dill weed, garlic salt and black pepper; pour over ham mixture.

3. Bake 30 to 35 minutes or until puffed and browned. Cut into wedges. Garnish with dill sprigs and lemon slices. *Makes 4 to 6 servings*

Delicious Ham & Cheese Puff Pie

Corned Beef Hash

2 large russet potatoes, peeled and cut into ½-inch cubes
½ teaspoon salt
¼ teaspoon black pepper
¼ cup (½ stick) butter or margarine
1 cup chopped onion
½ pound corned beef, finely chopped
1 tablespoon horseradish
4 eggs

1. Place potatoes in 10-inch skillet; cover with water. Bring to a boil over high heat. Reduce heat to low; simmer 6 minutes. (Potatoes will be firm.) Drain potatoes in colander; sprinkle with salt and pepper.

2. Melt butter in same skillet over medium heat. Add onion; cook and stir 5 minutes. Stir in corned beef, potatoes and horseradish; mix well. Press down mixture with spatula to flatten.

3. Reduce heat to low; cook 10 to 15 minutes. Turn mixture with spatula; pat down. Cook 10 to 15 minutes or until bottom is well browned.

4. Meanwhile, poach eggs. Top each serving with egg.   *Makes 4 servings*

Corned Beef Hash

Wake-Up Potato and Sausage Breakfast Casserole

1 pound kielbasa or smoked sausage, diced
1 cup chopped onion
1 cup chopped red bell pepper
1 package (20 ounces) Southwestern-style hash browns*
10 eggs
1 cup milk
1 cup (4 ounces) shredded Monterey Jack or sharp Cheddar cheese

Or substitute O'Brien potatoes; add ½ teaspoon chili powder.

Slow Cooker Directions

1. Coat slow cooker with nonstick cooking spray. Heat large skillet over medium-high heat. Add sausage and onion; cook and stir until sausage is browned. Drain fat. Stir in bell pepper.

2. Place one third of potatoes in slow cooker. Top with half of sausage mixture. Repeat layers, ending with potatoes.

3. Whisk eggs and milk in medium bowl. Pour evenly over potatoes. Cover; cook on LOW 6 to 7 hours.

4. Turn off slow cooker. Sprinkle with cheese; let stand 10 minutes or until cheese is melted. *Makes 8 servings*

Prep Time: 15 minutes • **Cook Time:** 6 to 7 hours (LOW)

Tip: For an attractive presentation, place this breakfast casserole on a serving platter. Run a rubber spatula around the outer edge of the casserole, lifting the bottom slightly. Invert onto a plate. Place a serving plate on top and invert again. Sprinkle with the cheese and let stand until cheese is melted.

Wake-Up Potato and Sausage Breakfast Casserole

Savory Sausage Bread Pudding

4 eggs

2 cups milk

¼ teaspoon *each* **salt, dried thyme and black pepper**

⅛ teaspoon crushed red pepper flakes

1 package (10 ounces) breakfast sausage links, cut into ½-inch pieces

2 cups day-old bread cubes, cut into ½-inch pieces

¾ cup (3 ounces) shredded Cheddar cheese

Slow Cooker Directions

1. Beat eggs in large bowl. Stir in milk, salt, thyme, black pepper and pepper flakes. Stir in sausage, bread and cheese. Press bread into egg mixture. Let stand 10 minutes or until bread has absorbed liquid.

2. Generously butter 2-quart baking dish that fits inside 5- or 6-quart slow cooker. Pour sausage mixture into dish. Cover dish with buttered foil, butter side down.

3. Pour 1 inch hot water into slow cooker. Add baking dish. Cover; cook on LOW 4 to 5 hours or until knife inserted into center comes out clean.

Makes 4 to 6 servings

Biscuit and Sausage Bake

2 cups biscuit baking mix

½ cup milk

1 egg

1 teaspoon vanilla

1 cup fresh or frozen blueberries

6 fully cooked breakfast sausage links, cut into small pieces

Warm maple syrup

1. Preheat oven to 350°F. Grease 8-inch square baking pan.

2. Whisk baking mix, milk, egg and vanilla in medium bowl. Fold in blueberries. Spread batter in prepared pan. Sprinkle with sausage.

3. Bake 22 minutes or until top is lightly browned. Cut into squares; serve with maple syrup.

Makes 6 servings

Savory Sausage Bread Pudding

Goat Cheese & Tomato Omelet

3 egg whites
2 eggs
1 tablespoon water
⅛ teaspoon salt
⅛ teaspoon black pepper
   Nonstick cooking spray
⅓ cup crumbled goat cheese
1 plum tomato, diced
2 tablespoons chopped fresh basil or parsley

1. Whisk together egg whites, eggs, water, salt and pepper in medium bowl.

2. Spray medium nonstick skillet with cooking spray; place over medium heat. Add egg mixture; cook 2 minutes or until eggs begin to set on bottom. Lift edges of omelet to allow uncooked portion of eggs to flow underneath. Cook 3 minutes or until center is almost set.

3. Sprinkle cheese, tomato and basil in center of omelet. Fold half of omelet over filling. Cook 1 to 2 minutes or until cheese begins to melt and center is set. Cut omelet in half; transfer to serving plates. *Makes 2 servings*

Prep Time: 10 minutes • **Cook Time:** 8 minutes

Goat Cheese & Tomato Omelet

Ham 'n' Apple Breakfast Casserole

1 package (15 ounces) refrigerated pie crusts (2 crusts)
1 pound thinly sliced ham, cut into bite-size pieces
1 can (about 21 ounces) apple pie filling
1 cup (4 ounces) shredded sharp Cheddar cheese
¼ cup plus 1 teaspoon sugar, divided
½ teaspoon ground cinnamon

1. Preheat oven to 425°F.

2. Place one crust in 9-inch pie pan, allowing edges to hang over sides. Arrange half of ham pieces in bottom; spoon apple pie filling over ham. Arrange remaining ham on top of apples; sprinkle with cheese.

3. Mix ¼ cup sugar and cinnamon in small bowl; sprinkle evenly over cheese. Arrange second crust over filling and crimp edges together. Brush crust lightly with water and sprinkle with remaining 1 teaspoon sugar. Cut slits for steam to escape.

4. Bake 20 to 25 minutes or until crust is golden brown. Cool 15 minutes before serving.   *Makes 6 servings*

This breakfast casserole can be assembled the night before, covered and refrigerated, then baked the next morning.

Ham 'n' Apple Breakfast Casserole

Summer Sausage Crustless Quiche

   4 eggs, lightly beaten
⅓ cup milk
¼ cup all-purpose flour
½ teaspoon baking powder
¼ teaspoon garlic powder
   2 cups (8 ounces) shredded Cheddar cheese, divided
1½ cups diced HILLSHIRE FARM® Summer Sausage
   1 cup cream-style cottage cheese with chives

Preheat oven to 375°F. Whisk eggs, milk, flour, baking powder and garlic powder in medium bowl until thoroughly combined. Stir in 1½ cups Cheddar cheese, sausage and cottage cheese.

Pour into greased 9-inch pie plate. Bake 25 to 30 minutes or until knife inserted into center comes out clean. Sprinkle with remaining ½ cup Cheddar cheese. Let stand 5 minutes, cut into 6 wedges and serve.   *Makes 6 servings*

Steak Hash

   2 tablespoons vegetable oil
   1 green bell pepper, chopped
½ medium onion, chopped
   2 russet potatoes (about 1 pound), baked and cut into bite-size
      pieces
½ pound cooked steak or roast beef, cut into 1-inch pieces
      Salt and black pepper
¼ cup (1 ounce) shredded Monterey Jack cheese
   4 eggs

1. Heat oil in large skillet over medium heat. Add bell pepper and onion; cook and stir until crisp-tender. Stir in potatoes; reduce heat to low. Cover; cook about 10 minutes or until potatoes are heated through, stirring occasionally.

2. Stir in steak; season with salt and black pepper. Sprinkle with cheese. Cover; cook 5 minutes or until steak is heated through and cheese is melted.

3. Meanwhile, poach eggs. Top each serving with egg.   *Makes 4 servings*

Summer Sausage Crustless Quiche

Apple and Granola Breakfast Cobbler

4 Granny Smith apples, peeled and sliced
2 cups granola cereal, plus additional for garnish
½ cup packed light brown sugar
2 tablespoons butter, cut into small pieces
1 tablespoon lemon juice
1 teaspoon ground cinnamon
   Cream, half-and-half or vanilla yogurt (optional)

Slow Cooker Directions

1. Combine apples, cereal, brown sugar, butter, lemon juice and cinnamon in slow cooker.

2. Cover; cook on LOW 6 hours or on HIGH 2 to 3 hours. Sprinkle with additional granola. Serve with cream, if desired.   *Makes 4 servings*

Prep Time: 5 minutes • **Cook Time:** 6 hours (LOW) or 2 to 3 hours (HIGH)

Apple and Granola Breakfast Cobbler

Pleasing Poultry

Homestyle Chicken & Biscuits

1 can (10¾ ounces) CAMPBELL'S® Condensed Cream of Chicken Soup (Regular or 98% Fat Free)

¼ cup milk

¾ cup shredded Cheddar cheese

¼ teaspoon ground black pepper

1 bag (16 ounces) frozen vegetable combination (broccoli, cauliflower, carrots), thawed

2 cans (4.5 ounces each) SWANSON® Premium Chunk Chicken Breast in Water, drained

1 package (7.5 ounces) refrigerated biscuits (10 biscuits)

1. Heat the oven to 400°F. Stir the soup, milk, cheese and black pepper in a 3-quart shallow baking dish. Stir in the vegetables and chicken.

2. Bake for 15 minutes or until the chicken mixture is hot and bubbling. Stir the chicken mixture.

3. Top the chicken mixture with the biscuits. Bake for 15 minutes or until the biscuits are golden brown.

Makes 4 servings

Prep Time: 15 minutes • **Bake Time:** 30 minutes

Kitchen Tip: Use the downtime while this one-dish meal is in the oven to make a fresh tomato salad. Slice some tomatoes and drizzle them with balsamic vinegar and olive oil.

Slow Cooker Chicken and Dressing

4 boneless skinless chicken breasts
  Salt and black pepper
4 slices Swiss cheese
2 cans (10¾ ounces each) condensed cream of chicken, celery or mushroom soup, undiluted
1 can (about 14 ounces) chicken broth
3 cups packaged stuffing mix
½ cup (1 stick) butter, melted

Slow Cooker Directions

1. Place chicken in slow cooker. Season with salt and pepper.

2. Top each chicken breast with cheese slice. Add soup and broth. Sprinkle stuffing mix over top; pour melted butter over all. Cover; cook on LOW 6 to 8 hours or on HIGH 3 to 4 hours. *Makes 4 servings*

Turkey Kielbasa with Cabbage, Sweet Potatoes and Apples

1 bottle (12 ounces) dark beer or ale
2 tablespoons Dijon mustard
½ teaspoon caraway seeds
6 cups coarsely shredded cabbage
1 pound fully cooked turkey kielbasa or smoked turkey sausage, cut into 2-inch pieces
1 Granny Smith apple, cut into ¼-inch wedges
1 can (16 ounces) sweet potatoes, cut into 1½-inch cubes

1. Combine beer, mustard and caraway seeds in large deep skillet. Bring to a boil over high heat. Add cabbage. Reduce heat to medium-low. Cover and cook 5 to 8 minutes or until cabbage is crisp-tender.

2. Add kielbasa, apple and sweet potatoes. Increase heat to high. Bring mixture to a boil. Reduce heat to medium-low. Cover and cook 3 to 5 minutes or until apple is crisp-tender and all ingredients are hot. *Makes 6 servings*

Favorite recipe from **National Turkey Federation**

Slow Cooker Chicken and Dressing

Old-Fashioned Turkey Pot Pie

1 package (18 ounces) JENNIE-O TURKEY STORE® SO EASY
Turkey Breast Chunks In Homestyle Gravy
1½ cups frozen mixed vegetables, thawed
⅛ teaspoon black pepper
1 package (15 ounces) refrigerated pie crust, divided

Preheat oven to 350°F.

In large bowl, combine turkey breast chunks in gravy, vegetables and pepper.

Place one pie crust in bottom and up side of 9-inch pie plate. Spoon turkey and vegetable mixture over crust. Place top crust over filling. Fold edges of crust inward and flute as desired to seal.

Bake 50 to 55 minutes or until crust is golden brown.

Cut into wedges and serve. *Makes 4 servings*

Broccoli, Turkey and Noodle Skillet

1 tablespoon butter
1 green bell pepper, chopped
1 cup frozen chopped broccoli, thawed
¼ teaspoon black pepper
1½ cups chicken broth
½ cup milk or half-and-half
2 cups diced cooked turkey breast
1 package (about 4 ounces) chicken and broccoli pasta mix
¼ cup sour cream

1. Melt butter in large skillet over medium-high heat. Add bell pepper, broccoli and black pepper; cook and stir 5 minutes or until bell pepper is crisp-tender. Add broth and milk; bring to a boil. Stir in turkey and pasta mix.

2. Reduce heat to low. Cook 8 to 10 minutes or until noodles are tender. Remove from heat. Stir in sour cream. Let stand, uncovered, 5 minutes or until sauce thickens. *Makes 4 servings*

Old-Fashioned Turkey Pot Pie

Zucchini, Chicken & Rice Casserole

Vegetable cooking spray

1 package (12 ounces) refrigerated or thawed frozen breaded cooked chicken tenders, cut into bite-sized strips

2 large zucchini, cut in half lengthwise and thinly sliced (about 4 cups)

1 jar (7 ounces) whole roasted sweet peppers, drained and thinly sliced

1 cup uncooked instant brown rice

1 can (10¾ ounces) CAMPBELL'S® Condensed Cream of Celery Soup (Regular or 98% Fat Free)

1 soup can water

½ cup sour cream

1. Heat the oven to 375°F. Spray a 3-quart shallow baking dish with the cooking spray.

2. Stir the chicken, zucchini, peppers and rice in the baking dish.

3. Stir the soup, water and sour cream in a small bowl. Pour the soup mixture over the chicken mixture. Cover the baking dish.

4. Bake for 35 minutes or until the rice is tender. Let stand for 10 minutes. Stir the rice before serving.   *Makes 4 servings*

Prep Time: 15 minutes • **Bake Time:** 35 minutes • **Stand Time:** 10 minutes

Kitchen Tip: Choose zucchini that have firm, dark green skin.

Zucchini, Chicken & Rice Casserole

Herbed Turkey Breast

1 can (10¾ ounces) CAMPBELL'S® Condensed Cream of
  Mushroom Soup (Regular or 98% Fat Free)
½ cup water
1 (4½- to 5-pound) turkey breast
1 teaspoon poultry seasoning
1 tablespoon chopped fresh parsley
  Hot mashed potatoes

Slow Cooker Directions

1. Stir the soup and water in a 3½- to 6-quart slow cooker. Rinse the turkey with cold water and pat it dry. Rub the turkey with the poultry seasoning and place it into the cooker. Sprinkle with the parsley.

2. Cover and cook on LOW for 8 to 9 hours* or until the turkey is cooked through. Let the turkey stand for 10 minutes before slicing. Serve with the soup mixture and mashed potatoes.   *Makes 8 servings*

Or on HIGH for 4 to 5 hours.

Prep Time: 10 minutes • **Cook Time:** 8 hours • **Stand Time:** 10 minutes

----

Choose turkey breasts that are plump and have no unpleasant odors. Always check the freshness date, which will indicate the last date the turkey breasts should be sold.

Herbed Turkey Breast

Southern BBQ Chicken and Rice

4 TYSON® Individually Frozen Chicken Half Breasts
1½ cups water
1 cup rice
1 cup barbecue sauce, divided
1 package (6 half ears) frozen corn on the cob (optional)

1. Wash hands. Combine chicken, water, rice and ³/₄ cup barbecue sauce in large skillet. Bring to a boil. Cover; reduce heat and simmer 25 minutes.

2. Add corn to skillet, if desired; cook 15 to 20 minutes longer or until internal juices of chicken run clear. (Or insert instant-read meat thermometer into thickest part of chicken. Temperature should read 180°F.)

3. Spoon remaining ¹/₄ cup barbecue sauce over chicken. Remove from heat; let stand 5 minutes or until liquid is absorbed. Refrigerate leftovers immediately.

Makes 4 servings

Cook Time: 55 minutes • **Total Time:** 60 minutes

Serving Suggestion: Serve with extra barbecue sauce and warm bread.

Southern BBQ Chicken and Rice

Turkey Pot Pie Casserole

Nonstick cooking spray
2 pounds turkey breast, cut into 1-inch cubes
6 tablespoons butter
⅓ cup all-purpose flour
½ teaspoon ground sage
½ teaspoon ground thyme
1½ cups chicken broth
1 cup milk
1 bag (16 ounces) frozen soup vegetables (carrots, potatoes, peas, celery, green beans, corn, onions and lima beans)
1 teaspoon salt
½ teaspoon black pepper
1 container (8 ounces) refrigerated crescent roll dough

1. Preheat oven to 375°F. Coat 13×9-inch baking dish with nonstick cooking spray.

2. Coat large nonstick skillet with cooking spray; heat over medium heat. Working in batches, brown turkey on all sides. Transfer to platter.

3. Melt butter in skillet. Whisk in flour, sage and thyme; cook and stir 5 minutes. Slowly whisk in broth and milk; cook, whisking constantly, about 5 minutes or until thickened.

4. Stir in turkey, vegetables, salt and pepper; cook 5 to 7 minutes, stirring frequently. Spoon mixture into prepared dish. Unroll crescent roll dough. Place over top of casserole. Bake 15 minutes or until top is golden brown.

Makes 6 servings

Turkey Pot Pie Casserole

Skillet Lasagna with Vegetables

½ pound Italian turkey sausage
½ pound ground turkey
2 stalks celery, sliced
⅓ cup chopped onion
2 cups marinara sauce
1⅓ cups water
4 ounces uncooked bow tie pasta
1 medium zucchini, halved lengthwise and cut into ½-inch-thick slices (2 cups)
¾ cup chopped green or yellow bell pepper
½ cup ricotta cheese
2 tablespoons finely shredded Parmesan cheese
½ cup (2 ounces) shredded mozzarella cheese

1. Remove sausage from casing. Cook and stir sausage, turkey, celery and onion in large skillet until turkey is no longer pink. Drain. Add marinara sauce and water; stir to combine. Bring to a boil. Add pasta; stir. Simmer, covered, 12 minutes.

2. Stir in zucchini and bell pepper. Simmer, covered, 2 minutes. Uncover; simmer 2 to 6 minutes or until vegetables are crisp-tender and desired consistency is reached.

3. Meanwhile, combine ricotta and Parmesan cheese in small bowl. Drop by rounded teaspoonfuls on top of mixture in skillet. Sprinkle with mozzarella cheese. Remove from heat; let stand, covered, 10 minutes.   *Makes 6 servings*

Prep and Cook Time: 30 minutes

Skillet Lasagna with Vegetables

Ham and Sage Stuffed Cornish Hens

1 cup plus 3 tablespoons sliced celery, divided

1 cup sliced leek

2 tablespoons butter, divided

¼ cup finely diced onion

¼ cup diced smoked ham

1 cup seasoned stuffing mix

1 cup chicken broth

1 tablespoon finely chopped fresh sage *or* 1 teaspoon ground sage

4 Cornish hens (about 1½ pounds each)

Salt and black pepper

Slow Cooker Directions

1. Coat 5- to 6-quart slow cooker with nonstick cooking spray. Toss 1 cup celery and leek in slow cooker.

2. Melt 1 tablespoon butter in large nonstick skillet over medium heat. Add remaining 3 tablespoons celery, onion and ham. Cook 5 minutes or until onion is translucent, stirring frequently. Stir in stuffing mix, broth and sage. Transfer mixture to medium bowl.

3. Rinse hens and pat dry; sprinkle with salt and pepper. Spoon stuffing into cavities; tie drumsticks together with kitchen twine.

4. Melt remaining 1 tablespoon butter in same skillet over medium-high heat. Place 2 hens, breast side down, in skillet and cook until browned on all sides. Transfer to slow cooker. Repeat with remaining hens.

5. Cover; cook on LOW 5 to 6 hours or on HIGH 3 to 4 hours. Remove and discard twine. Place hens on serving platter with vegetables; spoon broth over hens.

Makes 4 servings

Prep Time: 45 minutes • **Cook Time:** 5 to 6 hours (LOW) or 3 to 4 hours (HIGH)

Soups & Stews

Italian Skillet Roasted Vegetable Soup

1 tablespoon olive oil
1 red, yellow or orange bell pepper, chopped
1 clove garlic, minced
2 cups water
1 can (about 14 ounces) diced tomatoes
1 zucchini, thinly sliced
⅛ teaspoon red pepper flakes
1 can (about 15 ounces) navy beans, rinsed and drained
3 to 4 tablespoons chopped fresh basil
1 tablespoon olive oil
1 tablespoon balsamic vinegar
¾ teaspoon salt

1. Heat oil in Dutch oven over medium-high heat. Add bell pepper; cook and stir 4 minutes or until edges are browned. Add garlic; cook and stir 15 seconds. Add water, tomatoes, zucchini and pepper flakes. Bring to a boil over high heat. Reduce heat; cover and simmer 20 minutes.

2. Add beans, basil, oil, vinegar and salt. Remove from heat. Let stand, covered, 10 minutes before serving.

Makes 4 to 6 servings

Slow-Cooked Chicken and Mushroom Stew

4 TYSON® Individually Frozen Boneless Skinless Chicken Breasts

1 can (10.75 ounces) cream of mushroom and roasted garlic soup
    Salt and black pepper, to taste

8 ounces medium white mushrooms

1 cup baby-cut carrots

2 celery ribs, cut into 1½-inch lengths

Slow Cooker Directions

1. Stir together soup and ½ can of water in slow cooker. Wash hands. Cut chicken into 2-inch chunks. Sprinkle with salt and pepper to taste. Put chicken in slow cooker. Wash hands. Add mushrooms, carrots and celery. Stir gently to mix.

2. Cover and cook on LOW 6 to 8 hours or until internal juices of chicken run clear. (Or insert instant-read meat thermometer into thickest part of chicken. Temperature should read 180°F.) Refrigerate leftovers immediately.

Makes 4 servings

Prep Time: 10 minutes • **Cook Time:** 6 to 8 hours (LOW)

Serving Suggestion: Serve with hot rice sprinkled with parsley.

Peppery Potato Soup

2 cans (about 14 ounces each) chicken or vegetable broth
4 baking potatoes, halved and sliced crosswise
1 onion, quartered and sliced
1 stalk celery, sliced
½ teaspoon salt
½ teaspoon black pepper
1 cup half-and-half
¼ cup all-purpose flour
1 tablespoon butter
Celery leaves and fresh parsley (optional)

Slow Cooker Directions

1. Combine broth, potatoes, onion, celery, salt and pepper in slow cooker; mix well. Cover; cook on LOW 6 to 7½ hours.

2. Stir half-and-half into flour in medium bowl until smooth. Stir mixture into slow cooker. Cover; cook 1 hour.

3. Slightly mash with potato masher. Cook, uncovered, 30 minutes or until thickened. Just before serving, stir in butter. Garnish with celery leaves and parsley.

Makes 6 servings

Prep Time: 15 minutes • **Cook Time:** 7 to 8½ hours (LOW), plus 30 minutes

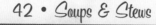

Peppery Potato Soup

Beef Stew with Bacon, Onion and Sweet Potatoes

1 pound beef stew meat, cut into 1-inch chunks
1 can (about 14 ounces) beef broth
2 sweet potatoes, peeled and cut into 2-inch pieces*
1 onion, cut into 1½-inch pieces
2 slices thick-cut bacon, diced
1 teaspoon dried thyme
1 teaspoon salt
¼ teaspoon black pepper
2 tablespoons cornstarch
2 tablespoons water

Or substitute 12 ounces carrots.

Slow Cooker Directions

1. Coat slow cooker with nonstick cooking spray. Combine beef, broth, sweet potatoes, onion, bacon, thyme, salt and pepper in slow cooker. Cover; cook on LOW 7 to 8 hours or on HIGH 4 to 5 hours.

2. Transfer beef and vegetables to serving bowl with slotted spoon; keep warm.

3. *Turn slow cooker to HIGH.* Stir cornstarch into water in small bowl until smooth. Stir into juices in slow cooker. Cook, uncovered, 15 minutes or until thickened, stirring occasionally. Return beef and vegetables to slow cooker. Cover; cook 15 minutes or until heated through. *Makes 4 servings*

Prep Time: 10 minutes • **Cook Time:** 7 to 8 hours (LOW) or 4 to 5 hours (HIGH), plus 30 minutes

Beef Stew with Bacon, Onion and Sweet Potatoes

Creamy Farmhouse Chicken and Garden Soup

½ **package (16 ounces) frozen pepper stir-fry vegetable mix**
1 **cup frozen corn, thawed**
1 **zucchini, sliced**
2 **bone-in chicken thighs, skinned***
1 **can (about 14 ounces) chicken broth**
½ **teaspoon minced garlic**
½ **teaspoon dried thyme**
2 **ounces uncooked egg noodles**
1 **cup half-and-half**
½ **cup frozen peas**
2 **tablespoons chopped fresh Italian parsley**
2 **tablespoons butter**
1 **teaspoon salt**
½ **teaspoon black pepper**

To skin chicken easily, grasp skin with paper towel and pull away. Repeat with fresh paper towel for each piece of chicken, discarding skins and towels.

Slow Cooker Directions

1. Combine stir-fry vegetables, corn and zucchini in slow cooker. Add chicken, broth, garlic and thyme. Cover; cook on HIGH 3 to 4 hours or until chicken is no longer pink in center. Remove chicken; cool slightly.

2. Add noodles to slow cooker. Cover; cook 20 minutes or until noodles are almost tender.

3. Meanwhile, debone and chop chicken. Return to slow cooker. Stir in half-and-half, peas, parsley, butter, salt and pepper. Let stand 5 minutes before serving. *Makes 4 servings*

Prep Time: 15 minutes • **Cook Time:** 3 to 4 hours (HIGH), plus 30 minutes

Jerk Turkey Stew

1 tablespoon vegetable oil
1 small red onion, chopped
1 clove garlic, minced
½ teaspoon ground ginger
¼ teaspoon salt
¼ teaspoon black pepper
⅛ to ¼ teaspoon ground red pepper*
⅛ teaspoon ground allspice
1 can (about 28 ounces) diced tomatoes
3 cups diced cooked turkey
2 cups cooked sweet potato (½-inch pieces)
½ cup turkey broth or gravy
1 tablespoon lime juice
1 tablespoon minced fresh chives

Use ⅛ teaspoon for a mildly hot dish; use ¼ teaspoon for a very hot dish.

1. Heat oil in Dutch oven over medium heat. Add onion and garlic; cook and stir 5 minutes. Add ginger, salt, black pepper, red pepper and allspice; cook 20 seconds. Stir in tomatoes, turkey, sweet potato and broth. Reduce heat to low; simmer 15 minutes.

2. Stir in lime juice; cover and let stand 10 minutes. Sprinkle with chives just before serving.
Makes 4 servings

Instead of sweet potatoes, try adding a cooked diced white potato or serving the stew over rice.

Jerk Turkey Stew

Potato Cheddar Soup

2 pounds new red potatoes, cut into ½-inch cubes
¾ cup coarsely chopped carrots
1 onion, coarsely chopped
½ teaspoon salt
3 cups chicken or vegetable broth
1 cup half-and-half
¼ teaspoon black pepper
2 cups (8 ounces) shredded Cheddar cheese

Slow Cooker Directions

1. Layer potatoes, carrots, onion and salt in slow cooker. Pour in broth. Cover; cook on LOW 6 to 7 hours or on HIGH 3 to 3½ hours or until vegetables are tender.

2. Stir in half-and-half and pepper. Cover; cook on HIGH 15 minutes. Turn off heat. Let stand, uncovered, 5 minutes. Stir in cheese until melted.

Makes 6 servings

Navy Bean & Ham Soup

6 cups water
5 cups dried navy beans, soaked overnight, rinsed and drained
1 pound ham, cubed
1 can (about 15 ounces) corn, drained
1 can (about 4 ounces) mild diced green chiles, drained
1 onion, diced
Salt and black pepper

Slow Cooker Directions

1. Place water, beans, ham, corn, chiles, onion, salt and pepper in slow cooker.

2. Cover; cook on LOW 8 to 10 hours or until beans are softened.

Makes 6 servings

Potato Cheddar Soup

Winter's Best Bean Soup

10 cups chicken broth

3 cans (about 15 ounces each) Great Northern beans, drained

1 can (about 14 ounces) diced tomatoes

6 ounces bacon, crisp cooked

1 large onion, chopped

1 package (about 10 ounces) frozen diced carrots

2 teaspoons minced garlic

1 teaspoon dried rosemary

1 teaspoon black pepper

Slow Cooker Directions

1. Combine all ingredients in slow cooker.

2. Cover; cook on LOW 8 hours.   *Makes 8 to 10 servings*

Beef Stew

1 medium onion, chopped (about ½ cup)

1 cup baby carrots

2 cups sliced celery

1 pound red potatoes, scrubbed and cubed

2 pounds beef stew meat, cut into chunks

2 teaspoons dried thyme leaves

1 can (14.5 ounces) HUNT'S® Diced Tomatoes

¾ cup water

1 can (6 ounces) HUNT'S® Tomato Paste

Slow Cooker Directions

1. Place onion in the bottom of 3½-quart or larger slow cooker. Add the following ingredients in this order: carrots, celery, potatoes and beef. Sprinkle with thyme. Pour diced tomatoes and water over the top of beef.

2. Cover; cook on LOW setting for 8 to 10 hours. Stir in tomato paste; cover. Cook an additional 10 minutes on HIGH setting.   *Makes 6 servings*

Hands On: 20 minutes • **Total Time:** 8 to 10 hours

Winter's Best Bean Soup

Veal Stew with Horseradish

1¼ pounds veal, trimmed and cut into 1-inch cubes

2 sweet potatoes, peeled and cut into 1-inch pieces

1 can (about 14 ounces) diced tomatoes

1 package (10 ounces) frozen corn

1½ cups frozen lima beans

1 onion, chopped

1 cup beef or vegetable broth

1 tablespoon chili powder

1 tablespoon prepared horseradish

1 tablespoon honey

Slow Cooker Directions

1. Combine veal, sweet potatoes, tomatoes, corn, beans, onion, broth, chili powder, horseradish and honey in slow cooker.

2. Cover; cook on LOW 7 to 8 hours or until veal is tender.

Makes 6 servings

Veal Stew with Horseradish

Irresistible Pork

Ham with Fruited Bourbon Sauce

1 (6-pound) bone-in ham
¾ cup packed dark brown sugar
½ cup raisins
½ cup apple juice
1 teaspoon ground cinnamon
¼ teaspoon red pepper flakes
⅓ cup dried cherries
¼ cup bourbon
¼ cup cornstarch

Slow Cooker Directions

1. Coat 5-quart slow cooker with nonstick cooking spray. Add ham, cut side up. Combine brown sugar, raisins, apple juice, cinnamon and pepper flakes in small bowl; stir well. Pour mixture evenly over ham. Cover; cook on LOW 9 to 10 hours or on HIGH 4½ to 5 hours. Add cherries 30 minutes before end of cooking time.

2. Transfer ham to cutting board. Let stand 15 minutes before slicing.

3. Pour cooking liquid into large measuring cup and let stand 15 minutes. Skim and discard fat. Return cooking liquid to slow cooker.

4. *Turn slow cooker to HIGH.* Stir bourbon into cornstarch in small bowl until smooth. Stir into cooking liquid. Cover; cook 15 minutes or until thickened. Serve sauce over ham. *Makes 10 to 12 servings*

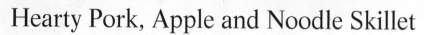

Hearty Pork, Apple and Noodle Skillet

2 apples, such as Fuji, Gala or Golden Delicious, peeled and cored
2 tablespoons butter, divided
1 onion, finely chopped
½ (27-ounce) package garlic and herb marinated pork loin fillet
1½ cups chicken broth
½ cup milk
1 package (about 4 ounces) stroganoff pasta mix
¼ teaspoon black pepper
¼ cup sour cream

1. Cut apples into ¼-inch-thick slices. Melt 1 tablespoon butter in large nonstick skillet over medium heat. Add apples and onion. Cook 5 to 10 minutes or until apples are lightly browned. Remove to large bowl; set aside.

2. Cut half of pork loin into ½-inch-thick slices. Melt remaining 1 tablespoon butter in same skillet over medium heat. Brown pork in batches, 2 to 3 minutes per side. Remove to plate; set aside.

3. Bring broth and milk to a boil in same skillet. Stir in pasta mix, apple mixture and pepper; reduce heat to medium. Cook 10 minutes or until noodles are tender and sauce is slightly thickened. Stir in sour cream. Serve pork over noodles. *Makes 4 servings*

Slow Cooked Pork & Sauerkraut

2 jars (32 ounces each) sauerkraut, rinsed and drained
2½ cups water
3 tablespoons brown mustard
1 package (about 1 ounce) dry onion soup mix
3 pounds boneless pork loin roast

Slow Cooker Directions

1. Combine sauerkraut, water, mustard and soup mix in slow cooker; mix well. Add pork to slow cooker.

2. Cover; cook on LOW 8 hours. Slice pork; serve with sauerkraut.

Makes 6 servings

Hearty Pork, Apple and Noodle Skillet

Best Ever Barbecued Ribs

1 teaspoon *each* salt, dried thyme and paprika
¼ teaspoon black pepper
⅛ teaspoon ground red pepper
3 to 3½ pounds well-trimmed pork baby back ribs, cut into 4 pieces
¼ cup ketchup
2 tablespoons brown sugar
1 tablespoon *each* Worcestershire sauce and soy sauce

Slow Cooker Directions

1. Coat slow cooker with nonstick cooking spray. Combine salt, thyme, paprika, black pepper and red pepper in small bowl; rub onto meaty side of ribs. Place ribs in slow cooker. Cover; cook on LOW 7 to 8 hours or on HIGH 3 to 4 hours.

2. Combine ketchup, brown sugar, Worcestershire sauce and soy sauce; mix well. Remove ribs from slow cooker; discard liquid. Coat ribs with sauce; return to slow cooker. Cook on HIGH 30 minutes.   *Makes 6 servings*

Kettle-Cooked Baked Beans with Smoked Sausage

1 package (2.1 ounces) fully cooked bacon, chopped
1 pound smoked sausage, sliced diagonally
1 medium onion, chopped (about ½ cup)
2 cans (31 ounces each) VAN CAMP'S® Pork and Beans
1 can (6 ounces) HUNT'S® Tomato Paste
½ cup HUNT'S® Ketchup
¼ cup packed brown sugar
2 tablespoons GULDEN'S® Spicy Brown Mustard

Slow Cooker Directions

1. Combine bacon, sausage, onion, beans, tomato paste, ketchup, sugar and mustard in slow cooker.

2. Cook on LOW setting for 4 to 6 hours or on HIGH setting for 2 to 3 hours. Stir before serving.   *Makes 8 servings*

Hands On: 10 minutes • **Total Time:** 4 to 6 hours (LOW)

Spicy Citrus Pork with Pineapple Salsa

1½ teaspoons ground cumin
½ teaspoon black pepper
¼ teaspoon salt
1½ pounds center-cut pork loin, rinsed and patted dry
1 tablespoon vegetable oil
2 cans (8 ounces each) pineapple tidbits* in juice, drained and
    ¼ cup juice reserved
2 tablespoons lemon juice, divided
1 teaspoon grated lemon peel
½ cup finely chopped orange or red bell pepper
2 tablespoons finely chopped red onion
1 tablespoon chopped fresh cilantro or mint
½ teaspoon grated fresh ginger (optional)
⅛ teaspoon red pepper flakes

*If tidbits are unavailable, purchase pineapple chunks and coarsely chop.

Slow Cooker Directions

1. Coat slow cooker with nonstick cooking spray. Combine cumin, black pepper and salt in small bowl. Rub evenly onto pork. Heat oil in medium skillet over medium-high heat. Cook pork 1 to 2 minutes per side. Transfer to slow cooker.

2. Spoon 2 tablespoons reserved pineapple juice and 1 tablespoon lemon juice over pork. Cover; cook on LOW 2 hours or on HIGH 1 hour or until meat thermometer registers 160°F and pork is barely pink in center.

3. Meanwhile, combine pineapple, remaining 2 tablespoons pineapple juice, remaining 1 tablespoon lemon juice, lemon peel, bell pepper, onion, cilantro, ginger, if desired, and pepper flakes in medium bowl. Toss gently to combine.

4. Transfer pork to serving platter. Let stand 10 minutes before slicing. Pour sauce evenly over pork. Serve with salsa. *Makes 6 servings*

Prep Time: 15 minutes • **Cook Time:** 2 hours (LOW) or 1 hour (HIGH)

Spicy Citrus Pork with Pineapple Salsa

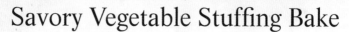

Savory Vegetable Stuffing Bake

¼ **pound bulk pork sausage**

1 **large onion, chopped**

½ **teaspoon dried thyme leaves, crushed**

1 **can (10¾ ounces) CAMPBELL'S® Condensed Cream of Celery Soup (Regular or 98% Fat Free)**

1 **cup stewed tomatoes**

2 **cups frozen vegetable combination (broccoli, corn, red pepper)**

3 **cups PEPPERIDGE FARM® Herb Seasoned Stuffing**

I. Cook the sausage, onion and thyme in a large skillet until the sausage is browned, stirring frequently to separate the meat. Pour off any fat.

2. Stir in the soup, tomatoes and vegetables in the skillet. Heat to a boil. Remove from the heat. Add the stuffing and stir lightly to coat. Spoon into 1½-quart baking dish.

3. Bake at 350°F. for 30 minutes or until hot.   *Makes 6 servings*

Prep Time: 20 minutes • **Bake Time:** 30 minutes

Savory Vegetable Stuffing Bake

Pork Chop Skillet Dinner

1 tablespoon olive oil or vegetable oil
4 bone-in pork chops, ¾-inch thick
1 medium onion, chopped (about ½ cup)
1 cup uncooked regular long-grain white rice
1 can (10½ ounces) CAMPBELL'S® Condensed Chicken Broth
1 cup orange juice
3 tablespoons chopped fresh parsley
4 orange slices

1. Heat the oil in a 10-inch skillet over medium-high heat. Add the pork and cook until it's well browned on both sides.

2. Add the onion and rice to the skillet and cook and stir until the rice is browned. Stir in the broth, orange juice and 2 tablespoons parsley and heat to a boil. Reduce the heat to low. Cover and cook for 20 minutes or until the pork is cooked through and the rice is tender.

3. Top with the orange slices and sprinkle with the remaining parsley.

Makes 4 servings

Prep Time: 10 minutes • **Cook Time:** 40 minutes

This skillet meal is great served
with a tossed green salad and chunky
applesauce for dessert.

Polska Kielbasa with Beer & Onions

18 ounces beer or brown ale

⅓ cup packed dark brown sugar

⅓ cup honey mustard

2 kielbasa sausages (16 ounces each), cut into 4-inch pieces

2 onions, quartered

Slow Cooker Directions

1. Combine beer, sugar and mustard in slow cooker. Add sausage pieces; top with onions.

2. Cover; cook on LOW 4 to 5 hours, stirring occasionally.

Makes 6 to 8 servings

Prep Time: 10 minutes • **Cook Time:** 4 to 5 hours (LOW)

Polska Kielbasa with Beer & Onions

Cajun-Style Country Ribs

2 cups baby carrots

1 onion, coarsely chopped

1 green bell pepper, cut into 1-inch pieces

1 red bell pepper, cut into 1-inch pieces

2 teaspoons minced garlic

2 tablespoons Cajun or Creole seasoning, divided

3½ to 4 pounds pork country-style ribs

1 can (about 14 ounces) stewed tomatoes, undrained

2 tablespoons water

1 tablespoon cornstarch

Hot cooked rice

Slow Cooker Directions

1. Combine carrots, onion, bell peppers, garlic and 2 teaspoons Cajun seasoning in 5-quart slow cooker; mix well.

2. Trim excess fat from ribs; cut into individual ribs. Sprinkle with 1 tablespoon Cajun seasoning; place in slow cooker. Pour tomatoes over ribs. Cover; cook on LOW 6 to 8 hours.

3. Remove ribs and vegetables from slow cooker with slotted spoon. Let liquid stand 15 minutes; skim off fat. Blend water, cornstarch and remaining 1 teaspoon Cajun seasoning in small bowl until smooth. Stir into slow cooker. *Turn slow cooker to HIGH.* Cook, uncovered, 15 minutes or until thickened. Return ribs and vegetables to sauce; carefully stir to coat. Serve with rice.

Makes 6 to 8 servings

Prep Time: 30 minutes • **Cook Time:** 6 to 8 hours (LOW), plus 15 minutes

Cajun-Style Country Ribs

Southern Pork Barbecue Dinner

1 tablespoon vegetable oil

½ cup chopped onion

½ cup chopped celery

½ cup chopped green bell pepper

1 container (about 18 ounces) refrigerated fully cooked shredded pork

1 can (about 15 ounces) pinto beans or black-eyed peas, rinsed and drained

1 can (8 ounces) tomato sauce

2 tablespoons Dijon mustard

1. Heat oil in large skillet over medium-high heat. Add onion, celery and bell pepper; cook and stir 5 minutes or until tender.

2. Reduce heat to low. Stir in pork, beans, tomato sauce and mustard; cook 5 to 10 minutes or until heated through. *Makes 4 to 6 servings*

Variation: To make sandwiches, omit the beans and serve the barbecued pork on buns.

Southern Pork Barbecue Dinner

Sweet 'n' Spicy Ribs

5 cups barbecue sauce

¾ cup packed brown sugar

¼ cup honey

2 tablespoons Cajun seasoning

1 tablespoon garlic powder

1 tablespoon onion powder

6 pounds pork ribs, cut into 3-rib or individual rib portions

Slow Cooker Directions

1. Stir together barbecue sauce, brown sugar, honey, Cajun seasoning, garlic powder and onion powder in medium bowl. Reserve 1 cup mixture for dipping sauce; refrigerate until ready to serve.

2. Place ribs in slow cooker. Pour remaining barbecue sauce mixture over ribs. Cover; cook on LOW 8 hours or until meat is very tender.

3. Serve ribs with reserved sauce.   *Makes 10 servings*

Prep Time: 10 to 15 minutes • **Cook Time:** 8 hours (LOW)

Sweet 'n' Spicy Ribs

Lemon Pork Chops

1 tablespoon vegetable oil
4 boneless pork chops
3 cans (about 8 ounces each) tomato sauce
1 onion, quartered and sliced (optional)
1 green bell pepper, cut into strips
1 tablespoon lemon-pepper seasoning
1 tablespoon Worcestershire sauce
2 lemons, quartered, divided

Slow Cooker Directions

1. Heat oil in large skillet over medium heat. Brown pork chops on both sides. Drain fat. Transfer pork chops to slow cooker.

2. Combine tomato sauce, onion, if desired, bell pepper, lemon-pepper seasoning and Worcestershire sauce in medium bowl. Add to slow cooker.

3. Squeeze juice from 4 lemon quarters over mixture; place squeezed lemon quarters into slow cooker. Cover; cook on LOW 6 to 8 hours. Remove cooked lemon wedges before serving. Serve pork with remaining 4 lemon quarters.

Makes 4 servings

Prep Time: 10 minutes • **Cook Time:** 6 to 8 hours (LOW)

Serving Suggestion: These pork chops are great served with green beans and couscous.

Company Slow Cooker Pork Chops

2 cans (10¾ ounces each) condensed cream of mushroom soup,
   undiluted
½ cup milk
1 package (3 ounces) cream cheese, softened
¼ cup sour cream
2 tablespoons oil
4 to 6 pork loin chops, cut ¾-inch thick
   Salt and black pepper
1 jar (2½ ounces) sliced dried beef
   Hot mashed potatoes

Slow Cooker Directions

1. Stir soup, milk, cream cheese and sour cream in medium bowl until smooth. Heat oil in large skillet over medium-high heat; brown both sides of pork chops. Season with salt and pepper.

2. Spray slow cooker with nonstick cooking spray. Place half of pork chops into slow cooker. Top with 4 slices dried beef. Pour half of sauce mixture over pork. Repeat with remaining chops, dried beef and sauce.

3. Cover; cook on LOW 8 to 9 hours. Serve with mashed potatoes.

Makes 4 to 6 servings

Bountiful Beef

Garlic Mashed Potatoes & Beef Bake

1 pound ground beef

1 can (10¾ ounces) CAMPBELL'S® Condensed Cream of
    Mushroom with Roasted Garlic Soup

1 tablespoon Worcestershire sauce

1 bag (16 ounces) frozen vegetable combination (broccoli,
    cauliflower, carrots), thawed

2 cups water

3 tablespoons butter

¾ cup milk

2 cups instant mashed potato flakes

1. Heat the oven to 400°F. Cook the beef in a 10-inch skillet over medium-high heat until it's well browned, stirring often to separate meat. Pour off any fat.

2. Stir the beef, ½ can soup, Worcestershire and vegetables in a 2-quart shallow baking dish.

3. Heat the water, butter and remaining soup in a 3-quart saucepan over medium heat to a boil. Remove the saucepan from the heat. Stir in the milk. Stir in the potatoes. Spoon the potatoes over the beef mixture.

4. Bake for 20 minutes or until the potatoes are lightly browned.

Makes 4 servings

Prep Time: 15 minutes • **Bake Time:** 20 minutes

Kitchen Tip: You can use your favorite frozen vegetable combination in this recipe.

Sauerbraten

2 cups cider vinegar

1 cup packed dark brown sugar

2 large onions, sliced (about 2 cups)

2 large carrots, cut into 2-inch pieces (about 1 cup)

10 gingersnap cookies, crushed

1 can (10½ ounces) CAMPBELL'S® Condensed Beef Consommé

Bouquet garni*

1 cup water

1 (4- to 5-pound) boneless beef rump roast

2 tablespoons vegetable oil

1 cup Burgundy wine

½ cup golden raisins

½ cup sour cream (optional)

Lay a 4-inch square of cheesecloth flat on the counter. Place ⅓ cup of pickling spice in the center of the cloth. Bring the corners of the cloth together and tie with kitchen string into a bundle.

Slow Cooker Directions

1. Heat the vinegar, brown sugar, onions, carrots, gingersnaps, consommé and bouquet garni in a 2-quart saucepan over medium-high heat to a boil. Remove from the heat. Stir in the water and let cool to room temperature.

2. Place the beef in a large nonmetallic bowl. Add the vinegar mixture and turn to coat. Cover and refrigerate for about 72 hours, turning the beef over in the marinade 1 to 2 times per day.

3. Remove the beef from the bowl and pat dry with paper towels. Reserve the marinade mixture. Heat the oil in a 12-inch skillet over medium-high heat. Add the beef and cook until it's well browned on all sides. Remove the beef from the skillet and place it into a 6-quart slow cooker.

4. Add the wine to the skillet and heat to a boil, stirring often. Pour the wine and reserved marinade over the beef.

5. Cover and cook on LOW for 7 to 8 hours or on HIGH for 4 to 5 hours. Stir in the raisins and the sour cream, if desired.   *Makes 6 servings*

Prep Time: 15 minutes • **Marinate Time:** 72 hours • **Cook Time:** 7 to 8 hours (LOW) or 4 to 5 hours (HIGH)

Baked Ziti

REYNOLDS WRAP® Non-Stick Foil
1 pound ground beef, browned and drained
4 cups (32-ounce jar) chunky garden-style pasta sauce
1 tablespoon Italian seasoning, divided
1 package (16 ounces) ziti pasta, cooked and drained
1 package (8 ounces) shredded mozzarella cheese, divided
1 container (16 ounces) ricotta cheese or cottage cheese
1 egg
¼ cup grated Parmesan cheese, divided

Preheat oven to 350°F.

Combine ground beef, pasta sauce and 2 teaspoons Italian seasoning. Stir pasta into meat sauce; spread half of mixture evenly in pan. Top with half of mozzarella cheese.

Combine ricotta cheese, egg, 2 tablespoons Parmesan cheese and remaining Italian seasoning; spread over mozzarella cheese in pan. Spread remaining pasta mixture over ricotta cheese mixture. Sprinkle with remaining mozzarella and Parmesan cheeses.

Cover with Reynolds Wrap Non-Stick Foil with non-stick (dull) side toward food.

Bake 45 minutes. Remove foil and continue baking 15 minutes or until cheese is melted and lightly browned. Let stand 15 minutes before serving.

Makes 8 servings

Prep Time: 20 minutes • **Cook Time:** 1 hour

Spiced Pot Roast

3 tablespoons packed brown sugar
2 teaspoons ground cloves
2 teaspoons ground allspice
2 teaspoons ground cinnamon
1 teaspoon cracked black pepper
1 (4-pound) boneless beef bottom round roast or beef chuck pot roast
2 cups SWANSON® Beef Stock
1 bottle (12 ounces) stout or dark beer
   Hot boiled potatoes
   Chopped fresh parsley (optional)

1. Stir the brown sugar, cloves, allspice, cinnamon and black pepper in a large bowl. Add the beef and turn to coat. Cover the bowl and refrigerate for 12 hours or overnight.

2. Place the beef in a 6-quart oven-safe saucepot. Pour the stock and beer over the beef. Cover the saucepot.

3. Bake at 350°F. for 3 hours or until the beef is fork-tender. Remove the beef from the saucepot and let stand for 10 minutes. Thinly slice the beef. Serve with the stock mixture and the potatoes. Sprinkle with the parsley, if desired.

Makes 8 servings

Prep Time: 5 minutes • **Marinate Time:** 12 hours • **Bake Time:** 3 hours • **Stand Time:** 10 minutes

Hearty Chili Macaroni

8 ounces small elbow macaroni, uncooked (2 cups)

1 pound ground sirloin beef

1 medium onion, chopped (about ½ cup)

1 can (15 ounces) red kidney beans, drained, rinsed

1 can (14.5 ounces) HUNT'S® Petite Diced Tomatoes with Mild Green Chilies, undrained

1 package (1.25 ounces) chili seasoning mix

1½ teaspoons granulated sugar

1. Cook macaroni according to package directions.

2. Brown meat with onions in a large skillet over medium-high heat while cooking macaroni; drain. Add beans, tomatoes with their liquid, chili seasoning and sugar; stir until well blended. Bring to a boil; cover. Reduce heat to low; simmer 10 minutes, stirring occasionally.

3. Drain macaroni; stir into meat mixture.   *Makes 6 servings (1½ cups each)*

Hands On: 20 minutes • **Total Time:** 20 minutes

Hearty Chili Macaroni

Sloppy Joe Casserole

1 pound ground beef

1 can (10¾ ounces) CAMPBELL'S® Condensed Tomato Soup (Regular or Healthy Request®)

¼ cup water

1 teaspoon Worcestershire sauce

⅛ teaspoon ground black pepper

1 package (7.5 ounces) refrigerated biscuits (10 biscuits)

½ cup shredded Cheddar cheese

1. Heat the oven to 400°F. Cook the beef in a 10-inch skillet over medium-high heat until it's well browned, stirring often to separate meat. Pour off any fat.

2. Stir the soup, water, Worcestershire and black pepper in the skillet and heat to a boil. Spoon the beef mixture into a 1½-quart casserole. Arrange the biscuits around the inside edge of the casserole. Bake for 15 minutes or until the biscuits are golden brown. Sprinkle the cheese over the beef mixture.

Makes 5 servings

Prep Time: 15 minutes • **Bake Time:** 15 minutes

Beefy Pasta Skillet

1 pound ground beef

1 medium onion, chopped (about ½ cup)

1 can (10¾ ounces) CAMPBELL'S® Condensed Tomato Soup (Regular or Healthy Request®)

¼ cup water

1 tablespoon Worcestershire sauce

½ cup shredded Cheddar cheese

2 cups cooked corkscrew-shaped pasta (rotini) or elbow pasta

1. Cook the beef and onion in a 10-inch skillet over medium-high heat until the beef is well browned, stirring often to separate the meat. Pour off any fat.

2. Stir the soup, water, Worcestershire, cheese and pasta in the skillet and cook until the mixture is hot and bubbling.

Makes 4 servings

Prep Time: 5 minutes • **Cook Time:** 15 minutes

Sloppy Joe Casserole

Skillet Franks and Potatoes

1 package (16 ounces each) HEBREW NATIONAL® Quarter
  Pound Dinner Beef Franks
3 tablespoons PURE WESSON® Vegetable Oil, divided
4 medium red potatoes, chopped, cooked and drained
  (about 3 cups)
1 large onion, chopped (about 1 cup)
1 medium green bell pepper, chopped (about 1 cup)
1 teaspoon ground dried sage
½ teaspoon salt
¼ teaspoon ground black pepper
2 tablespoons chopped fresh parsley (optional)

Make shallow cuts in franks (no more than halfway through) about every inch. Heat 1 tablespoon of the oil in large nonstick skillet over medium heat. Add franks; heat 5 minutes or until browned, turning occasionally. Remove franks from skillet; set aside.

Add the remaining 2 tablespoons oil, potatoes, onion and bell pepper to same skillet. Cook and stir 12 minutes or until potatoes are golden brown. Stir in sage, salt and pepper; mix well.

Return franks to skillet. Cook 5 minutes or until heated through, turning franks once halfway through cooking time. Sprinkle with parsley, if desired.

Makes 4 servings

Hands On: 40 minutes • **Total Time:** 40 minutes

Skillet Franks and Potatoes

Home-Style Shepherd's Pie

8 ounces ground beef

8 ounces Italian sausage, casings removed

1 cup chopped onion

2 cups frozen mixed vegetables, thawed

1 cup water

1 can (about 6 ounces) tomato paste

¼ cup chopped fresh Italian parsley

1 tablespoon beef bouillon granules

2 teaspoons sugar

¼ teaspoon salt

¼ teaspoon black pepper

⅛ teaspoon ground red pepper

1 package (2 pounds) refrigerated mashed potatoes

1½ cups (6 ounces) shredded sharp Cheddar cheese

½ cup chopped green onions

1. Preheat oven to 350°F. Coat 12×8-inch baking dish with nonstick cooking spray.

2. Brown beef and sausage 6 to 8 minutes in large nonstick skillet over medium high, stirring to break up meat. Drain all but 1 tablespoon fat. Add onion; cook and stir 2 minutes or until translucent. Add vegetables, water, tomato paste, parsley, bouillon, sugar, salt, black pepper and red pepper; stir until well blended.

3. Transfer mixture to prepared baking dish. Spoon potatoes evenly over mixture. Sprinkle with cheese and green onions. Coat sheet of foil with cooking spray; place over dish, sprayed side down. Bake 22 to 25 minutes or until bubbly.

Makes 8 servings

Sausage, Beef & Bean Casserole

1 pound sweet or hot Italian pork sausage, cut into 1-inch pieces
½ pound ground beef
1 small onion, chopped (about ¼ cup)
1 bag (6 ounces) fresh baby spinach leaves
1 can (10¾ ounces) CAMPBELL'S® Condensed Cream of
    Mushroom Soup (Regular or 98% Fat Free)
¼ cup milk
1 can (about 15 ounces) white kidney beans (cannellini), rinsed and
    drained
1 cup PEPPERIDGE FARM® Herb Seasoned Stuffing
½ cup crumbled blue cheese or shredded Cheddar cheese

1. Cook the sausage, beef and onion in a 12-inch nonstick skillet or 5-quart saucepot until the meats are well browned, stirring often to separate the meat. Pour off any fat. Add the spinach and cook until the spinach wilts.

2. Stir the soup, milk and beans into the skillet. Spoon the mixture into a 2-quart casserole.

3. Stir the stuffing and cheese in a small bowl. Sprinkle around the edge of the dish.

4. Bake at 350°F. for 30 minutes or until hot and bubbly and the internal temperature of the sausage mixture is 160°F.   *Makes 6 servings*

Prep Time: 10 minutes • **Bake Time:** 30 minutes

Sausage, Beef & Bean Casserole

Tomato Beef Stroganoff

2½ pounds boneless chuck roast, cut into large chunks
1 can (28 ounces) HUNT'S® Crushed Tomatoes
1 can (8 ounces) HUNT'S® Tomato Sauce
1 can (6 ounces) HUNT'S® Tomato Paste
1 package (6 ounces) sliced fresh mushrooms
2 packages (1.5 ounces each) beef stroganoff seasoning mix
2 cups egg noodles, uncooked
1 cup sour cream

Slow Cooker Directions

1. Combine roast, tomatoes, tomato sauce, tomato paste, mushrooms and seasoning mix in slow cooker. Cook on LOW setting for 8 hours or on HIGH setting for 4 hours until meat is tender.

2. Stir in noodles the last 20 minutes of cook time and cook for remainder of time on HIGH setting. Stir in sour cream before serving.

Makes 8 servings (1 cup each)

Hands On: 10 minutes • **Total Time:** 8 hours (LOW) or 4 hours (HIGH)

Contents

Chilis & Chowders

Chicken and Three-Pepper Corn Chowder

12 TYSON® Individually Frozen Boneless Skinless Chicken Tenderloins, thawed, cut into bite-size pieces
2 tablespoons butter or margarine
3 cups frozen pepper and onion stir-fry mixture
1 large clove garlic, minced
2 cups frozen corn
1 cup chicken broth
⅛ teaspoon ground red pepper
2 cups (8 ounces) shredded or diced pasteurized process cheese product
½ cup whipping cream
1 tablespoon chopped fresh cilantro

1. Wash hands. In large skillet, melt butter over medium heat. Add frozen vegetables; cook and stir 5 to 7 minutes or until tender. Add garlic; stir 30 seconds. Remove vegetables and set aside.

2. Add chicken tenders, corn, broth and red pepper to skillet; bring to a boil. Reduce heat; cover and simmer 5 minutes. Over medium heat, add cheese and cream to chicken mixture. Cook and stir until cheese is melted and internal juices of chicken run clear. (Or insert instant-read meat thermometer into thickest part of chicken. Temperature should read 180°F.) Stir in chopped cilantro.

3. Ladle into individual bowls. Refrigerate leftovers. *Makes 4 servings*

Cook Time: 25 minutes

Idaho Potato Chili

1 pound Idaho Potatoes, peeled and cut into ½-inch cubes
    (about 2½ cups)
1 tablespoon vegetable oil
1 large onion, chopped (about 1 cup)
1 green bell pepper, diced (about 1 cup)
1 clove garlic, minced
8 ounces ground turkey
2 tablespoons chili powder
1 can (28 ounces) whole tomatoes, undrained
1 can (16 ounces) kidney beans, drained and rinsed
1 cup water
½ teaspoon salt
¼ cup chopped fresh cilantro
¼ cup plain nonfat yogurt *or* 2 tablespoons low-fat sour cream
¼ cup sliced green onions or chopped tomato (optional)

1. Heat oil in large saucepan over medium-high heat. Add onion, pepper and garlic. Cook and stir 5 minutes or until softened.

2. Add turkey. Cook and stir 5 to 6 minutes or until no longer pink, breaking up with spoon.

3. Stir in chili powder. Cook for 1 minute. Add canned tomatoes with juice, potatoes, beans, water and salt. Bring to a boil. Reduce heat to low. Simmer, covered, 30 minutes, stirring occasionally.

4. Remove from heat. Stir in cilantro. Top with yogurt and green onions, if desired.

Makes 4 to 6 servings

Favorite recipe from **Idaho Potato Commission**

Idaho Potato Chili

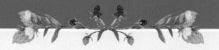

Bacon-Ham Chowder

1 cup radiatore or other small shape pasta
½ pound sliced bacon
4 chicken bouillon cubes
2 cups water
5 small potatoes, cubed (about 5 cups)
1 bunch green onions, chopped
1 cup sliced carrots
4 cups whole milk
½ cup all-purpose flour
1½ cups cubed cooked ham
1 tablespoon hot pepper sauce
  Cracked black pepper, to taste
1 cup shredded Cheddar cheese

Cook pasta according to package directions until tender but firm; do not overcook.

Cook bacon until crisp and set aside. When cool, crumble into bite-size pieces. Combine bouillon and water in large pan; heat to boiling. Add potatoes; cover and simmer 5 minutes.

Add onions and carrots and simmer until vegetables are tender, about 10 to 12 minutes. Whisk milk and flour together; add to vegetables. Cook over medium heat, stirring frequently until bubbly and thickened. Add ham, bacon, pepper sauce, cracked pepper, pasta and cheese; heat until cheese is melted.

Makes 6 servings

Favorite recipe from **North Dakota Wheat Commission**

Hearty Chicken Chili

1 onion, finely chopped
1 jalapeño pepper,* minced
1 clove garlic, minced
1½ teaspoons chili powder
¾ teaspoon salt
½ teaspoon ground cumin
½ teaspoon dried oregano
½ teaspoon black pepper
¼ teaspoon red pepper flakes (optional)
1½ pounds boneless skinless chicken thighs, cut into 1-inch pieces
2 cans (about 15 ounces each) hominy, rinsed and drained
1 can (about 15 ounces) pinto beans, rinsed and drained
1 cup chicken broth
1 tablespoon all-purpose flour (optional)
Chopped fresh parsley or fresh cilantro (optional)

Jalapeño peppers can sting and irritate the skin, so wear rubber gloves when handling peppers and do not touch your eyes.

Slow Cooker Directions

1. Combine onion, jalapeño, garlic, chili powder, salt, cumin, oregano, black pepper and red pepper flakes, if desired, in slow cooker.

2. Add chicken, hominy, beans and broth. Stir well to combine. Cover; cook on LOW 7 hours.

3. For thicker chili, stir 1 tablespoon flour into 3 tablespoons cooking liquid in small bowl. Stir into slow cooker. *Turn slow cooker to HIGH.* Cover; cook 10 minutes or until thickened. Garnish with parsley. *Makes 6 servings*

Prep Time: 15 minutes • **Cook Time:** 7 hours (LOW), plus 10 minutes

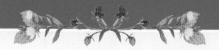

Corn and Buttermilk Blender Chowder

3 cups buttermilk, chilled and divided

2 cups corn

3 green onions, coarsely chopped

1½ tablespoons coarsely chopped fresh cilantro, plus additional for garnish

¼ teaspoon salt

⅛ teaspoon black pepper

1. Combine 1 cup buttermilk, corn, green onions, 1½ tablespoons cilantro, salt and pepper in blender. Pulse until corn and green onions are minced. Pour mixture into pitcher; stir in remaining 2 cups buttermilk.

2. Serve immediately or refrigerate up to 4 hours. Stir well before serving. Garnish with additional cilantro. *Makes 4 servings*

Head-'Em-Off-at-the-Pass White Chili

1 tablespoon olive oil

½ cup chopped onion

2 cans (15 ounces each) cannellini beans, undrained

1 jar (11 ounces) NEWMAN'S OWN® Bandito Salsa, divided

1½ cups chopped cooked chicken

½ cup chicken broth

1 teaspoon oregano leaves

½ teaspoon celery salt

1½ cups (6 ounces) shredded mozzarella cheese, divided

Heat oil in 2-quart saucepan; add onion and cook and stir until tender. Stir in beans, ½ cup of Newman's Own® Bandito Salsa, chicken, chicken broth, oregano and celery salt. Cover; simmer over medium heat 10 minutes, stirring occasionally. Just before serving, stir in 1 cup of mozzarella cheese. Divide chili evenly among serving bowls. Top each with a portion of remaining mozzarella and salsa. *Makes 4 servings*

Corn and Buttermilk Blender Chowder

Hearty Corn Chowder

PAM® Original No-Stick Cooking Spray
1 package (46 ounces) frozen Banquet® Crock-Pot Classics®
Chicken with Red Skin Potatoes and Vegetables
1¾ cups vegetable broth
1 bag (16 ounces) frozen whole kernel corn
1 can (12 ounces) evaporated milk
12 slices bacon, cooked and crumbled

Slow Cooker Directions

1. Spray insert of 4-quart slow cooker with cooking spray.

2. Thaw sauce pouch according to package directions. Place potato pouch on plate in refrigerator. Pour sauce into slow cooker; add vegetable broth in place of water and stir until dissolved.

3. Stir in chicken and vegetables from package plus corn. Cover and cook on LOW 8 to 10 hours (for shorter cooking time, cook on HIGH 4 hours).

4. About 35 minutes before serving, add refrigerated potatoes and evaporated milk. Stir to blend; cover and cook the remaining 35 minutes.

5. Serve immediately and top each serving with crumbled bacon.

Makes 8 servings

Hands On: 5 minutes • **Total Time:** 8 to 10 hours

Keep the lid on! Slow cookers can take up to 30 minutes to regain heat lost when the cover is removed. Only remove it when instructed to do so by the recipe.

Hearty Corn Chowder

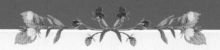

Smokin' Texas Chili

2 tablespoons olive oil

1½ pounds boneless beef sirloin steak or top round steak, ¾-inch thick, cut into ½-inch pieces

1 medium onion, chopped (about ½ cup)

2 cloves garlic, minced

3 cups PACE® Chunky Salsa, any variety

½ cup water

1 tablespoon chili powder

1 teaspoon ground cumin

1 can (about 15 ounces) red kidney beans, rinsed and drained

¼ cup chopped fresh cilantro leaves

Chili Toppings (optional)

1. Heat 1 tablespoon oil in a 6-quart saucepot over medium-high heat. Add the beef in 2 batches and cook until it's well browned, stirring often. Remove the beef from the saucepot.

2. Add the remaining oil and heat over medium heat. Add the onion and cook until it's tender. Add the garlic and cook for 30 seconds.

3. Add the salsa, water, chili powder and cumin. Heat to a boil. Return the beef to the saucepot. Stir in the beans. Reduce the heat to low. Cover and cook for 1 hour. Uncover and cook for 30 minutes or until the beef is fork-tender.

4. Sprinkle with the cilantro and Chili Toppings, if desired.

Makes 6 servings

Prep Time: 15 minutes • **Cook Time:** 2 hours

Chili Toppings: Chopped tomatoes, chopped onions, sour cream and/or shredded cheese.

Smokin' Texas Chili

Double Corn Chowder

1 cup corn
1 cup canned hominy
6 ounces Canadian bacon, chopped
2 stalks celery, chopped
1 onion or shallot, chopped
1 jalapeño pepper,* seeded and minced
¼ teaspoon salt
¼ teaspoon dried thyme
¼ teaspoon black pepper
1 cup chicken broth
1 tablespoon all-purpose flour
1½ cups milk,** divided

*Jalapeño peppers can sting and irritate the skin, so wear rubber gloves when handling peppers and do not touch your eyes.

**For richer chowder, use ¾ cup milk and ¾ cup half-and-half.

Slow Cooker Directions

1. Combine corn, hominy, bacon, celery, onion, jalapeño, salt, thyme and black pepper in slow cooker. Add broth. Cover; cook on LOW 5 to 6 hours or on HIGH 3 to 3½ hours.

2. Stir flour into 2 tablespoons milk in small bowl until smooth; stir into slow cooker. Whisk in remaining milk. Cover; cook on LOW 20 minutes or until slightly thickened and heated through. *Makes 4 servings*

Prep Time: 10 minutes • **Cook Time:** 5 to 6 hours (LOW) or 3 to 3½ hours (HIGH), plus 20 minutes

Double Corn Chowder

Super Chili for a Crowd

2 large onions, chopped
1 tablespoon minced garlic
2 pounds boneless top round or sirloin steak, cut into ½-inch cubes
1 pound ground beef
1 can (28 ounces) crushed tomatoes in purée
1 can (15 to 19 ounces) red kidney beans, undrained
⅓ cup *Frank's® RedHot®* Original Cayenne Pepper Sauce
2 packages (1¼ ounces each) chili seasoning mix

1. Heat 1 tablespoon oil in 5-quart saucepot or Dutch oven until hot. Sauté onions and garlic until tender; transfer to bowl.

2. Heat 3 tablespoons oil in same pot; cook meat in batches until well browned. Drain fat.

3. Add ¾ cup water and remaining ingredients to pot. Stir in onion and garlic. Heat to boiling, stirring. Simmer, partially covered, for 1 hour or until meat is tender, stirring often. Garnish as desired.   *Makes 10 servings*

Prep Time: 15 minutes • **Cook Time:** 1 hour, 15 minutes

Best Ever Chili

1½ pounds ground beef
1 cup chopped onion
2 cans (about 15 ounces each) kidney beans, drained and 1 cup liquid reserved
1½ pounds plum tomatoes, diced
1 can (about 15 ounces) tomato paste
3 to 6 tablespoons chili powder

Slow Cooker Directions

1. Brown beef and onion 6 to 8 minutes in large skillet over medium heat, stirring to break up meat. Drain fat. Transfer to slow cooker.

2. Add beans, bean liquid, tomatoes, tomato paste and chili powder; mix well. Cover; cook on LOW 10 to 12 hours.   *Makes 8 servings*

Super Chili for a Crowd

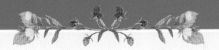

Country Chicken Chowder

   2 tablespoons butter
1½ pounds chicken tenders, cut into ½-inch pieces
   2 onions, chopped
   2 stalks celery, sliced
   2 carrots, sliced
   2 cups frozen corn
   2 cans (10¾ ounces each) cream of potato soup, undiluted
1½ cups chicken broth
   1 teaspoon dried dill weed
   ½ cup half-and-half

Slow Cooker Directions

1. Melt butter in large skillet. Add chicken; cook until browned. Transfer to slow cooker. Top with onions, celery, carrots, corn, soup, broth and dill.

2. Cover; cook on LOW 3 to 4 hours. Turn off heat; stir in half-and-half. Cover; let stand 5 to 10 minutes or until heated through.   *Makes 8 servings*

Creamy Roasted Garlic & Potato Chowder

   2 cups 1% milk
1½ cups water
   1 tablespoon HERB-OX® chicken flavored bouillon
   1 cup refrigerated diced potatoes
   ½ cup frozen whole kernel corn, thawed
   ¼ cup light roasted garlic flavored cream cheese
1¼ cups instant mashed potato flakes
   ¼ cup *each* shredded Cheddar cheese and sliced green onions
   ¼ cup crumbled HORMEL® fully cooked bacon or HORMEL® real bacon bits

In saucepan, bring milk, water, bouillon and refrigerated potatoes to a boil. Reduce heat and simmer for 5 to 8 minutes or until potatoes are tender. Stir in corn, cream cheese and instant potato flakes. Heat over low heat until warmed through. Ladle chowder into bowls. Top with cheese, green onions and bacon.

Makes 4 servings

Country Chicken Chowder

Hearty Beef and Bean Chili

2½ pounds boneless chuck roast, cut into large chunks
1 can (28 ounces) HUNT'S® Whole Peeled Tomatoes
1 can (6 ounces) HUNT'S® Tomato Paste
1 can (30 ounces) beans in chili seasoned sauce
1 package (1.25 ounces) chili seasoning mix

Slow Cooker Directions

Combine roast, tomatoes, tomato paste, beans and seasoning mix in slow cooker.

Cover; cook on LOW for 8 to 10 hours or on HIGH for 4 to 6 hours until meat is tender. *Makes 8 servings*

Hands On: 5 minutes • **Total Time:** 8 to 10 hours (LOW) or 4 to 6 hours (HIGH)

Do not use the slow cooker to reheat leftover food. Transfer cooled leftovers to a resealable food storage bag or plastic storage container with a tight-fitting lid and refrigerate. Use a microwave oven or the stove for reheating.

Hearty Beef and Bean Chili

Savory Breads

Confetti Scones

  2 teaspoons olive oil
  $\frac{1}{3}$ cup *each* minced red bell pepper and green bell pepper
  $\frac{1}{2}$ teaspoon dried thyme
  1 cup all-purpose flour
  $\frac{1}{4}$ cup whole wheat flour
$1\frac{1}{2}$ teaspoons baking powder
  $\frac{1}{2}$ teaspoon baking soda
  $\frac{1}{2}$ teaspoon sugar
  $\frac{1}{4}$ teaspoon ground red pepper
  $\frac{1}{8}$ teaspoon salt
  $\frac{1}{3}$ cup sour cream
  $\frac{1}{3}$ cup milk
  $\frac{1}{4}$ cup grated Parmesan cheese
  2 tablespoons minced green onion

1. Preheat oven to 400°F. Line baking sheets with parchment paper; set aside.

2. Heat oil in small skillet over medium heat. Add bell peppers and thyme; cook and stir 5 minutes or until tender.

3. Combine flours, baking powder, baking soda, sugar, ground red pepper and salt in large bowl. Add sour cream, milk, Parmesan, green onion and bell pepper mixture; mix to form sticky dough. *Do not overmix.*

4. Drop dough by rounded tablespoonfuls onto prepared baking sheets. Place in oven and immediately reduce heat to 375°F. Bake 13 to 15 minutes or until golden. Remove to wire rack; cool completely. *Makes 24 scones*

Wild Rice Three Grain Bread

1 package active dry yeast
⅓ cup warm water (105° to 115°F)
2 cups milk, scalded and cooled to 105° to 115°F
½ cup honey
2 tablespoons butter, melted
2 teaspoons salt
4 to 4½ cups bread flour or unbleached all-purpose flour
2 cups whole wheat flour
½ cup rye flour
½ cup uncooked rolled oats
1 cup cooked wild rice
1 egg, beaten with 1 tablespoon water
½ cup hulled sunflower seeds

In large bowl, dissolve yeast in water. Add milk, honey, butter and salt. Stir in 2 cups bread flour, whole wheat flour, rye flour and oats to make a soft dough. Add wild rice; cover and let rest 15 minutes. Stir in enough additional bread flour to make a stiff dough. Turn dough out onto board and knead 10 minutes. Add more flour as necessary to keep dough from sticking. Turn dough into lightly greased bowl; turn dough over to coat. Cover and let rise until doubled, about 2 hours. Punch down dough. Knead briefly on lightly oiled board. To shape dough, divide into 3 portions; roll into long strands. Braid strands and place on greased baking sheet in wreath shape, or divide in half and place each half in greased 9½×5½-inch loaf pans. Let rise until doubled, about 45 minutes. Brush tops of loaves with egg mixture; slash loaves if desired. Sprinkle with sunflower seeds. Bake at 375°F 45 minutes or until loaves sound hollow when tapped. *Makes 1 braided wreath or 2 loaves*

Favorite recipe from **Minnesota Cultivated Wild Rice Council**

Wild Rice Three Grain Bread

Sausage and Cheddar Corn Bread

   1 tablespoon vegetable oil
   $^1/_2$ pound bulk pork sausage
   1 onion, diced
   1 jalapeño pepper,* diced
   1 package (8 ounces) corn muffin mix
   1 cup (4 ounces) shredded Cheddar cheese, divided
   $^1/_3$ cup milk
   1 egg

*Jalapeño peppers can sting and irritate the skin, so wear rubber gloves when handling peppers and do not touch your eyes.

1. Heat oil in large cast iron skillet over medium heat. Brown sausage, stirring to break up meat. Add onion and jalapeño; cook and stir 5 minutes or until vegetables are softened. Remove sausage mixture to medium bowl.

2. Preheat oven to 350°F. Combine corn muffin mix, $^1/_2$ cup cheese, milk and egg in separate medium bowl. Pour batter into skillet. Spread sausage mixture over top. Sprinkle with remaining $^1/_2$ cup cheese.

3. Bake 20 to 25 minutes or until edges are lightly browned. Cut into wedges. Refrigerate leftovers. *Makes 10 servings*

Popovers

   1 cup all-purpose flour, plus additional for muffin cups
   1 cup milk
   3 eggs
   1 tablespoon butter, softened
   $^1/_2$ teaspoon salt

1. Preheat oven to 375°F. Grease and flour 12 standard ($2^1/_2$-inch) muffin cups.

2. Place 1 cup flour, milk, eggs, butter and salt in food processor or blender; process $2^1/_2$ minutes.

3. Pour batter into prepared cups, filling each about three-fourths full. Bake 45 to 50 minutes or until golden brown and crispy. *Makes 12 popovers*

Sausage and Cheddar Corn Bread

Basic White Bread

2 cups warm water (105° to 115°F)
2 packages active dry yeast
2 tablespoons sugar
6 to 6½ cups all-purpose flour, divided
½ cup nonfat dry milk powder
2 tablespoons shortening
2 teaspoons salt

1. Combine water, yeast and sugar in large bowl. Let stand 5 minutes or until bubbly.

2. Add 3 cups flour, milk powder, shortening and salt; beat with electric mixer at low speed until blended. Increase speed to medium; beat 2 minutes. Stir in enough additional flour, about 3 cups to make soft dough. Turn out onto lightly floured surface. Knead about 10 minutes, adding enough remaining flour to make dough smooth and elastic.

3. Shape dough into ball; place in large greased bowl. Turn dough to grease top. Cover with clean kitchen towel; let rise in warm place about 1 hour or until doubled in size.

4. Punch down dough; knead on lightly floured surface 1 minute. Cover with towel; let rest 10 minutes.

5. Grease 2 (8×4-inch) loaf pans. Divide dough in half. Roll out half of dough into 12×8-inch rectangle with lightly floured rolling pin. Starting with 1 short side, roll up dough jelly-roll style. Pinch seam and ends to seal. Place loaf, seam side down, in prepared pan, tucking ends under. Repeat with remaining dough. Cover and let rise in warm place 1 hour or until doubled in size.

6. Preheat oven to 375°F. Bake 30 to 35 minutes or until loaves are golden brown and sound hollow when tapped. Immediately remove from pans; cool completely on wire racks.

Makes 2 loaves

Basic White Bread

Farmer-Style Sour Cream Bread

- 1 cup sour cream, at room temperature
- 3 tablespoons water
- 2½ to 3 cups all-purpose flour, divided
- 1 package active dry yeast
- 2 tablespoons sugar
- 1½ teaspoons salt
- ¼ teaspoon baking soda
- Vegetable oil
- 1 tablespoon poppy or sesame seeds

1. Stir together sour cream and water in small saucepan. Heat over low heat until temperature reaches 120° to 130°F. *Do not boil.* Combine 2 cups flour, yeast, sugar, salt and baking soda in large bowl. Stir sour cream mixture into flour mixture until well blended. Turn out dough onto lightly floured surface. Knead about 5 minutes, adding enough remaining flour until dough is smooth and elastic.

2. Grease large baking sheet. Shape dough into ball; place on prepared baking sheet. Flatten into 8-inch circle. Brush top with oil and sprinkle with poppy seeds. Invert large bowl over dough and let rise in warm place 1 hour or until doubled in size.

3. Preheat oven to 350°F. Bake 22 to 27 minutes or until golden brown. Remove immediately from baking sheet; cool on wire rack.

Makes 8 to 12 servings

Farmer-Style Sour Cream Bread

Onion Buckwheat Bread

1 pound diced white onions
3 tablespoons olive oil
4½ teaspoons yeast
1½ cups water, at 90°F
½ cup milk
6½ cups unbleached bread flour
½ cup buckwheat flour
5 teaspoons sea salt
1 tablespoon finely chopped fresh rosemary
¾ cup (3 ounces) shredded Gouda or Cheddar cheese
Unbleached bread flour as needed for kneading
4 tablespoons poppy seeds or nigella seeds (onion seeds)

1. Sauté onions in olive oil in large skillet over medium-high heat until just browned, about 5 minutes. Set aside to cool.

2. Combine yeast with water in large bowl; let sit 10 minutes until bubbly.

3. Add milk to yeast mixture; stir to combine. Gradually add bread flour, buckwheat flour, salt, rosemary and onions to yeast mixture. When mixture is well combined, add cheese and blend. The dough will be slightly sticky.

4. Knead dough on lightly floured surface about 10 minutes until smooth and elastic. Add additional bread flour as needed if dough is too soft.

5. Lightly oil clean bowl. Place dough in bowl; cover and let rise until doubled in bulk, 1½ to 2 hours.

6. Gently punch down dough and place on lightly floured surface. Cut dough in half and shape into round loaves. Spritz top of each loaf with water and press on poppy seeds or nigella seeds. Place on lightly floured baking sheet; cover and let rise until almost doubled in bulk, 45 minutes to 1 hour.

7. Preheat oven to 450°F. Slash tops of loaves with sharp knife and place in oven. Add steam by placing 2 ice cubes in pan on bottom of oven. Bake 10 minutes. Reduce heat to 400°F and bake an additional 35 to 40 minutes. Cool loaves completely on rack. *Makes 2 (10-inch) round loaves*

Favorite recipe from **National Onion Association**

Onion Buckwheat Bread

Freezer Rolls

1¼ cups warm water (100° to 110°F)
2 envelopes FLEISCHMANN'S® Active Dry Yeast
½ cup sugar
½ cup warm milk (100° to 110°F)
⅓ cup butter or margarine, softened
1½ teaspoons salt
5½ to 6 cups all-purpose flour
2 large eggs

Place ½ cup warm water in large bowl. Sprinkle yeast over water; stir until dissolved. Add remaining ¾ cup warm water, sugar, warm milk, butter, salt and 2 cups flour. Beat 2 minutes at medium speed of electric mixer. Add eggs and ½ cup flour. Beat at high speed for 2 minutes. Stir in enough remaining flour to make soft dough. Turn out onto lightly floured surface. Knead until smooth and elastic, about 8 to 10 minutes. Cover with plastic wrap; let rest for 20 minutes.

Punch dough down. Shape into desired shapes for dinner rolls. Place on greased baking sheets. Cover with plastic wrap and foil, sealing well. Freeze up to 1 week.* Once frozen, rolls may be placed in plastic freezer bags.

Remove rolls from freezer; unwrap and place on greased baking sheets. Cover; let rise in warm, draft-free place until doubled in size, about 1½ hours.

Bake at 350°F for 15 minutes or until done. Remove from baking sheets; cool on wire racks. *Makes about 2 dozen rolls*

*To bake without freezing: After shaping, let rise in warm, draft-free place until doubled in size, about 1 hour. Bake according to above directions.

Shaping the Dough: Crescents: Divide dough in half; roll each half to 14-inch circle. Cut each circle into 12 pie-shaped wedges. Roll up tightly from wide end. Curve ends slightly to form crescents. Knots: Divide dough into 24 equal pieces; roll each into 9-inch rope. Tie once loosely. Coils: Divide dough into 24 equal pieces; roll each into 9-inch rope. Coil each rope and tuck end under the coil. Twists: Divide dough into 24 equal pieces; roll each into 12-inch rope. Fold each rope in half and twist three to four times. Pinch ends to seal.

Freezer Rolls

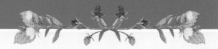

Roasted Garlic Breadsticks

1 large head garlic, roasted*
1 tablespoon butter, softened
1 cup warm water (110° to 120°F)
1 package active dry yeast
1 teaspoon sugar
2½ to 3 cups all-purpose flour, divided
1 teaspoon salt
1 tablespoon olive oil
1 egg white
1 tablespoon water
1 tablespoon sesame seeds

*To roast garlic, preheat oven to 400°F. Remove outer layers of papery skin and cut ¼ inch off top of garlic head. Place cut side up on a piece of heavy-duty foil. Drizzle with 2 teaspoons olive oil; wrap in foil. Bake 25 to 30 minutes or until cloves are soft. Cool slightly. Squeeze garlic pulp from skins.

1. Combine garlic and butter in small bowl. Cover and set aside.

2. Combine warm water, yeast and sugar in large bowl; let stand 5 minutes or until bubbly. Beat in 1½ cups flour, salt and oil into yeast mixture with electric mixer at low speed until blended. Increase speed to medium; beat 2 minutes. Stir in enough additional flour to make soft dough.

3. Turn out dough onto lightly floured surface. Knead about 5 minutes, adding enough remaining flour until dough is smooth and elastic. Shape dough into ball; place in large greased bowl. Turn dough to grease top. Cover; let rise in warm place about 1 hour or until doubled in size.

4. Punch down dough; knead on floured surface 1 minute. Cover; let rest 10 minutes. Grease 2 large baking sheets. Roll dough into 12-inch square with floured rolling pin; spread with garlic mixture. Fold square in half. Roll dough into 14×7-inch rectangle; cut crosswise into 7×1-inch strips.

5. Holding ends of each strip, twist 3 to 4 times. Place strips 2 inches apart on prepared baking sheets, pressing both ends to seal. Cover; let rise in warm place about 30 minutes or until doubled in size.

6. Preheat oven to 400°F. Combine egg white and water in small bowl. Brush breadsticks with egg white mixture. Sprinkle with sesame seeds. Bake 20 to 22 minutes or until golden. *Makes 12 breadsticks*

Roasted Garlic Breadsticks

French Bread

2½ cups warm water (105° to 115°F), divided
2 packages active dry yeast
1 tablespoon sugar
6¾ to 7½ cups bread or all-purpose flour, divided
2 teaspoons salt
2 tablespoons yellow cornmeal

1. Combine ½ cup warm water, yeast and sugar in large bowl; let stand 5 minutes or until bubbly. Add 2 cups flour, remaining 2 cups warm water and salt. Beat with electric mixer at low speed until blended. Increase speed to medium; beat 2 minutes. Stir in enough additional flour, about 4¾ cups, to make soft dough.

2. Turn out onto lightly floured surface. Knead about 10 minutes, adding enough remaining flour until dough is smooth and elastic. Shape dough into ball; place in large greased bowl. Turn dough to grease top. Cover with clean kitchen towel; let rise in warm place 1 to 1½ hours or until doubled in size.

3. Punch down dough. Knead dough in bowl 1 minute. Cover with towel; let rise in warm place about 1 hour or until doubled in size. Grease 2 large baking sheets. Sprinkle with cornmeal; set aside.

4. Punch down dough. Turn out dough onto lightly floured surface; knead several times to remove air bubbles. Cut dough into 4 pieces. Cover with towel; let rest 10 minutes. Roll each piece of dough back and forth, forming loaf about 14 inches long and 2 inches in diameter. Place loaves 4 inches apart on prepared baking sheets. Cut 3 (¼-inch-deep) slashes into each loaf with sharp knife. Brush loaves with water. Cover with towel; let rise in warm place about 35 minutes or until doubled in bulk.

5. Place small baking pan in bottom of oven. Preheat oven to 450°F. Place 2 ice cubes in pan. Brush loaves with water; bake 10 minutes. Rotate baking sheets top to bottom. Quickly spray loaves with cool water using spray mister. Reduce heat to 400°F; bake 10 to 15 minutes more or until loaves are golden brown. Immediately remove from baking sheets; cool on wire racks. Serve warm.

Makes 4 loaves

French Bread

Main Dishes

Roasted Chicken & Vegetables

1 REYNOLDS® Oven Bag, Large Size
1 tablespoon flour
2 cloves garlic, minced
2 tablespoons *each* olive oil and fresh lemon juice
2 teaspoons dried Italian seasoning
1 whole chicken (3½ to 4 pounds)
2 cups peeled baby carrots, halved lengthwise
1 medium red bell pepper, cut in cubes
1 medium onion, cut in small wedges
   Seasoned salt and black pepper to taste

PREHEAT oven to 350°F.

SHAKE flour in Reynolds Oven Bag; place in 13×9×2-inch baking pan.

ADD garlic, olive oil, lemon juice and Italian seasoning to oven bag. Turn bag to mix with flour. Place chicken in bag. Turn bag to coat chicken with olive oil mixture. Arrange vegetables around chicken. Sprinkle seasoned salt and pepper over chicken and vegetables.

CLOSE oven bag with nylon tie; cut six ½-inch slits in top. Tuck ends of bag in pan.

BAKE 50 to 60 minutes or until meat thermometer reads 180°F.

Makes 4 to 6 servings

Prep Time: 20 minutes • **Cook Time:** 50 minutes

Peppered Steaks with Caramelized Onions

2 beef shoulder center steaks (Ranch steaks), cut 1 inch thick (about 8 ounces each)

2 teaspoons seasoned pepper blend

Caramelized Onions and Sautéed Spinach (recipe follows)

Roasted Potatoes:

1 pound unpeeled small red and brown-skinned potatoes, quartered

1 teaspoon olive oil

½ teaspoon dried thyme

⅛ teaspoon salt

1. Preheat oven to 425°F. Place potatoes on rimmed baking sheet. Sprinkle with oil, thyme and salt; toss to coat. Roast in oven 30 to 40 minutes or until tender, turning occasionally.

2. Meanwhile, press pepper blend onto beef steaks. Heat large nonstick skillet over medium heat until hot. Place steaks in skillet, cook 13 to 16 minutes for medium rare (145°F) to medium (160°F) doneness, turning twice.

3. Carve steaks; season with salt as desired. Top with onions; serve with potatoes and spinach.   *Makes 4 servings*

Caramelized Onions and Sautéed Spinach: Heat 1 tablespoon butter in large nonstick skillet over medium heat until melted. Add 1 large yellow onion, cut ¼ inch thick; cook 18 to 21 minutes or until caramelized, stirring frequently. Remove onion from skillet; keep warm. Heat 2 teaspoons olive oil and 1 large clove minced garlic over medium heat in same skillet about 30 seconds or until fragrant. Add 8 cups spinach and ⅛ teaspoon salt. Toss to coat and cook 1 minute or until just wilted, stirring frequently. Serve immediately.

Prep and Cook Time: 45 minutes to 1 hour

Favorite recipe **Courtesy The Beef Checkoff**

Peppered Steak with Caramelized Onions

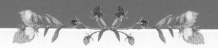

Almond-Crusted Salmon with Thyme & Lemon Butter Sauce

¼ cup plain dry bread crumbs
¼ cup blanched almonds
1 clove garlic
2 tablespoons olive oil
8 salmon fillets (about 3 pounds)
1 tablespoon cornstarch
1½ cups SWANSON® Chicken Stock
2 tablespoons lemon juice
1 teaspoon chopped fresh thyme leaves or ¼ teaspoon dried thyme leaves, crushed
3 tablespoons butter
¼ cup chopped shallot or onion

1. Place the bread crumbs, almonds and garlic into a food processor or blender. Cover and process until the mixture is finely ground. Gradually pour in the olive oil while the food processor is running and process until the mixture is moist.

2. Place the salmon into a roasting pan. Top the salmon with the bread crumb mixture and press to adhere.

3. Bake at 400°F. for 15 minutes or until the salmon flakes easily when tested with a fork and the bread crumb mixture is golden. Remove the salmon from the oven and keep warm.

4. Stir the cornstarch, stock, lemon juice and thyme in a medium bowl until the mixture is smooth.

5. Heat 2 tablespoons butter in a 1-quart saucepan over medium heat. Add the shallots and cook until they're tender. Stir in the cornstarch mixture and heat to a boil. Cook and stir until the sauce boils and thickens. Add the remaining butter and cook and stir until it's melted. Serve the salmon with the sauce.

Makes 8 servings

Prep Time: 15 minutes • **Bake Time:** 15 minutes

Almond-Crusted Salmon with Thyme & Lemon Butter Sauce

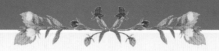

Beef Wellington

1 (2- to 2½-pound) beef tenderloin
   Ground black pepper (optional)
**½ (17.3-ounce) package PEPPERIDGE FARM® Puff Pastry Sheets
   (1 sheet)**
1 egg
1 tablespoon water
1 tablespoon butter
2 cups finely chopped mushrooms
1 medium onion, finely chopped (about ½ cup)

1. Heat the oven to 425°F. Place the beef in a lightly greased roasting pan. Season with the black pepper, if desired. Roast for 30 minutes or until a meat thermometer reads 130°F. Cover the pan and refrigerate for 1 hour.

2. Thaw the pastry sheet at room temperature for 40 minutes or until it's easy to handle. Heat the oven to 425°F. Beat the egg and water in a small bowl with a fork.

3. Heat the butter in a 10-inch skillet over medium-high heat. Add the mushrooms and onion and cook until the vegetables are tender and all the liquid is evaporated, stirring often.

4. Unfold the pastry sheet on a lightly floured surface. Roll the pastry sheet into a rectangle 4 inches longer and 6 inches wider than the beef. Brush the pastry sheet with the egg mixture. Spoon the mushroom mixture onto the pastry sheet to within 1 inch of the edges. Place the beef in the center of the mushroom mixture. Starting at the long sides, fold the pastry over the beef. Place seam-side down on a baking sheet. Tuck the ends under to seal. Brush the pastry with the egg mixture.

5. Bake for 25 minutes or until the pastry is golden and a meat thermometer reads 140°F. Slice and serve warm.   *Makes 10 servings*

Thaw Time: 40 minutes • **Prep Time:** 30 minutes • **Chill Time:** 1 hour •
Bake Time: 25 minutes

Beef Wellington

Sweet & Spicy Petite Sirloin Steaks with Vegetable Barley "Risotto"

   1 pound boneless beef top sirloin steak, cut ¾ inch thick
   ½ cup ready-to-serve beef broth
   ¼ cup balsamic vinegar
   2 tablespoons jalapeño pepper jelly
      Vegetable Barley "Risotto" (recipe follows)

Seasoning:
   ¾ teaspoon garlic salt
   ¾ teaspoon chili powder
   ½ teaspoon coarse grind black pepper
   ¼ teaspoon ground cumin
   ¼ teaspoon dried oregano leaves

1. Prepare Vegetable Barley "Risotto."

2. Meanwhile, cut beef steak crosswise into four equal "petite" steaks. Combine seasoning ingredients; press evenly into both sides of each steak. Heat large nonstick skillet over medium heat until hot. Place steaks in skillet; cook about 8 to 10 minutes for medium rare (145°F) to medium (160°F) doneness, turning once. Remove steaks; keep warm.

3. Add broth, vinegar and jelly to skillet; cook until browned bits attached to skillet are dissolved and sauce thickens slightly, about 3 to 5 minutes. Spoon sauce over steaks and serve with barley "risotto."   *Makes 4 servings*

Vegetable Barley "Risotto"

   ¾ cup quick-cooking barley
   1 cup coarsely chopped zucchini
   ¼ cup minced shallots
   2 teaspoons olive oil
   1 clove garlic, minced
   1 can (14 to 14½ ounces) ready-to-serve beef broth
   ¾ cup chopped tomatoes
   ¼ teaspoon pepper

continued on page 146

Sweet & Spicy Petite Sirloin Steak with Vegetable Barley "Risotto"

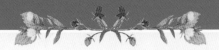

1. Heat large nonstick Dutch oven over medium heat until hot. Add barley and cook, stirring until lightly toasted, about 5 minutes. Add zucchini, shallots, oil and garlic; cook about 3 minutes until zucchini is crisp and tender.

2. Stir in ³/₄ cup of broth. Bring to a simmer. Cook 5 minutes until liquid is almost absorbed. Add remaining broth; return to simmer and continue cooking 7 to 9 minutes or until barley is tender. Stir in tomatoes and pepper.

Makes 4 servings

Prep and Cook Time: 50 minutes

Favorite recipe **Courtesy The Beef Checkoff**

The most common form of barley is pearled, meaning that it has been polished many times to remove the bran and most of the germ. Pearled barley is available in a quick-cooking form and can be found in most supermarkets.

Roasted Turkey Breast with Herbed Au Jus

1 tablespoon all-purpose flour
1 plastic oven bag, turkey size
1 cup SWANSON® Chicken Stock
½ teaspoon *each* ground dried sage leaves, dried rosemary and thyme leaves, crushed
1 (6- to 8-pound) bone-in turkey breast
½ teaspoon paprika (optional)
1 can (10½ ounces) CAMPBELL'S® Turkey Gravy

1. Add the flour to the oven bag. Close and shake the bag to distribute the flour. Place the bag in a 13×9×2-inch baking pan. Add the stock, sage, rosemary and thyme to the bag. Squeeze the bag to blend in the flour.

2. Rinse the turkey with cold water and pat dry with a paper towel. Sprinkle the turkey evenly with the paprika. Add the turkey to the bag. Close the bag with the nylon tie. Cut 6 (½-inch) slits in the top of the bag. Insert a meat thermometer through a slit in the bag into the thickest part of the meat, making sure the thermometer is not touching the bone.

3. Roast the turkey at 350°F. for 1¾ to 2 hours.* Begin checking for doneness after 1½ hours of roasting time. Let the turkey stand for 10 minutes before slicing.

4. Remove the turkey from the bag. Pour the turkey liquid from the bag into a large cup. Skim off the fat.

5. Heat the turkey liquid and gravy in a 2-quart saucepan over medium heat until hot. Serve with the turkey.   *Makes 6 servings*

*The internal temperature of the turkey should reach 170°F.

Prep Time: 10 minutes • **Cook Time:** 2 hours • **Stand Time:** 10 minutes

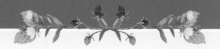

Southern Fried Catfish with Hush Puppies

Hush Puppy Batter (recipe follows)
4 catfish fillets (about 1½ pounds)
½ cup yellow cornmeal
3 tablespoons all-purpose flour
1½ teaspoons salt
¼ teaspoon ground red pepper
Vegetable oil

1. Prepare Hush Puppy Batter; set aside.

2. Rinse catfish; pat dry with paper towels. Combine cornmeal, flour, salt and red pepper in shallow dish. Dip fish into cornmeal mixture. Heat 1 inch oil in large heavy skillet over medium heat until 375°F on deep-fry thermometer.

3. Cook fish in batches 4 to 5 minutes or until golden brown and fish begins to flake when tested with fork. Drain fish on paper towels. Allow temperature of oil to return to 375°F between batches.

4. To make Hush Puppies, drop batter by tablespoonfuls into hot oil. Cook in batches 2 minutes or until golden brown. Drain on paper towels.

Makes 4 servings

Hush Puppy Batter

1½ cups yellow cornmeal
½ cup all-purpose flour
2 teaspoons baking powder
½ teaspoon salt
1 cup milk
1 onion, minced
1 egg, lightly beaten

1. Combine cornmeal, flour, baking powder and salt in medium bowl. Add milk, onion and egg. Stir until well blended.

2. Allow batter to stand 5 to 10 minutes before frying.

Makes about 24 hush puppies

Southern Fried Catfish with Hush Puppies

Cherry & Mushroom Stuffed Pork Chops

2 tablespoons vegetable oil, divided
1 cup chopped fresh shiitake mushrooms
¼ cup finely chopped onion
¼ cup finely chopped celery
¼ cup dried sweetened cherries, chopped
¼ teaspoon salt
⅛ teaspoon dried thyme
⅛ teaspoon black pepper
4 boneless pork loin chops (about 1¼ pounds), cut 1 inch thick
1 teaspoon all-purpose flour
¼ cup chicken broth
¼ cup cherry juice

1. Heat 1 tablespoon oil in 12-inch skillet. Add mushrooms, onion and celery; cook and stir over medium-high heat 4 minutes. Stir in cherries, salt, thyme and pepper. Remove from heat.

2. Make deep pocket in side of each pork chop; fill with one fourth of cherry stuffing. Skewer pockets closed with toothpicks.

3. Heat remaining 1 tablespoon oil in same skillet over medium heat. Add pork chops. Brown over medium heat 7 to 8 minutes per side or until cooked through.

4. Remove pork from skillet. Pour off fat. Add flour to skillet; cook 30 seconds, stirring constantly. Stir in broth and juice, scraping up browned bits from bottom of skillet. Cook 1 minute to thicken sauce slightly.

5. Return pork chops to skillet and turn to coat evenly. Serve pork with sauce.

Makes 4 servings

Cherry & Mushroom Stuffed Pork Chop

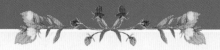

Pesto Meatballs with Spaghetti

   1 pound ground turkey
   ⅓ cup plain dry bread crumbs
   ¼ cup grated Parmesan cheese
   ¼ cup milk
   2 teaspoons dried basil
   ½ teaspoon garlic powder
   ½ teaspoon black pepper
   1 tablespoon olive oil
   1 can (about 14 ounces) stewed tomatoes
1½ cups chopped mushrooms
   1 green bell pepper, chopped
   ½ cup chopped onions
   6 cups hot cooked spaghetti

1. Combine turkey, bread crumbs, cheese, milk, basil, garlic powder and black pepper in large bowl; mix well. Shape into 24 meatballs.

2. Heat oil in nonstick skillet over medium-high heat. Add tomatoes, mushrooms, bell pepper and onions; simmer 5 to 6 minutes or until softened. Add meatballs to skillet in 2 batches; cook 5 to 6 minutes or until browned on all sides. Cook additional 10 to 15 minutes or until cooked through.

3. Serve meatballs and sauce over spaghetti.   *Makes 6 servings*

To quickly shape uniform meatballs, place the turkey mixture on a cutting board and pat evenly into large square, 1 inch thick. Cut into 1-inch squares and shape each into a ball.

Pesto Meatballs with Spaghetti

Crusted Tilapia Florentine

1 egg
2 teaspoons water
1 cup Italian-seasoned dry bread crumbs
4 fresh tilapia fillets (about 4 ounces each)
2 tablespoons olive oil
2⅔ cups PREGO® Traditional Italian Sauce
2 cups frozen chopped spinach
Hot cooked noodles

1. Beat the egg and water with a fork in a shallow dish. Place the bread crumbs on a plate. Dip the fish in the egg mixture, then coat with the bread crumbs.

2. Heat the oil in a 12-inch skillet over medium-high heat. Add the fish and cook for 8 minutes, turning once or until the fish flakes easily when tested with a fork. Remove the fish and keep warm.

3. Stir the Italian sauce and spinach into the skillet. Heat to a boil. Reduce the heat to medium. Cook for 2 minutes or until the spinach is wilted. Serve the sauce over the fish. Serve with the noodles. *Makes 4 servings*

Prep Time: 10 minutes • **Cook Time:** 15 minutes

Crusted Tilapia Florentine

On the Side

Macaroni and Cheese with Mixed Vegetables

2 tablespoons all-purpose flour
1¼ cups milk, divided
½ cup (2 ounces) shredded sharp Cheddar cheese
½ cup shredded Parmesan cheese
1½ cups frozen mixed vegetables, cooked and drained
1⅓ cups cooked whole wheat elbow macaroni, rotini or penne
¼ teaspoon salt
⅛ teaspoon black pepper

1. Preheat oven to 325°F. Coat 1½-quart baking dish with nonstick cooking spray.

2. Stir flour into ¼ cup milk in medium saucepan until smooth. Add remaining milk; stir until well blended. Cook, stirring constantly, over medium heat until thickened.

3. Combine cheeses in separate medium bowl. Stir half of cheese mixture into saucepan. Add vegetables, macaroni, salt and pepper.

4. Spoon macaroni mixture into prepared baking dish. Sprinkle with remaining cheese. Bake 20 minutes or until cheese melts and macaroni is heated through. Let stand 5 minutes before serving. *Makes 4 servings*

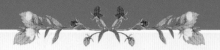

Corny Corn Fritters

- 2 cups vegetable oil
- 1 package (12-count) ORTEGA® Taco Shells
- ¾ cup all-purpose flour
- 2 teaspoons baking powder
- ½ teaspoon baking soda
- 2 eggs
- 1 cup milk
- 1 cup frozen whole-kernel corn, thawed
  ORTEGA® Black Bean & Corn Salsa

Heat oil in medium saucepan over medium-high heat to 375°F. Line platter with paper towels.

Place taco shells in resealable plastic bag; close bag. Crush with rolling pin until finely ground. Place crumbs in medium bowl. Add flour, baking powder and baking soda; mix well.

Combine eggs and milk in small bowl; mix well. Pour egg mixture into dry ingredients; mix well. Fold in corn. Let stand 10 minutes.

Place heaping tablespoonfuls of mixture into hot oil. Cook 4 minutes or until golden brown. Remove with slotted spoon. Drain on paper towels. Serve with salsa for dipping.   *Makes about 30 fritters*

Prep Time: 15 minutes • **Start to Finish:** 20 minutes

Tip: For cheesy corn fritters, add 1 cup finely shredded Cheddar cheese to the fritter mixture along with the egg mixture.

Corny Corn Fritters

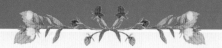

Cheesy Green Bean Casserole

¾ cup milk

2 teaspoons all-purpose flour

1 teaspoon dried minced onion

½ teaspoon black pepper

1 package (16 ounces) frozen cut green beans, thawed

1 cup (4 ounces) shredded Cheddar cheese, divided

¼ cup seasoned dry bread crumbs

1. Preheat oven to 350°F.

2. Whisk milk, flour, dried onion and pepper in medium bowl until well blended. Pour into 1½-quart baking dish. Stir in green beans and ½ cup cheese.

3. Bake, uncovered, 25 minutes. Sprinkle with remaining ½ cup cheese and bread crumbs. Bake 5 minutes or until cheese is melted.   *Makes 6 servings*

Potatoes au Gratin

4 to 6 unpeeled baking potatoes (about 2 pounds)

2 cups (8 ounces) shredded Cheddar cheese

1 cup (4 ounces) shredded Swiss cheese

2 tablespoons butter

3 tablespoons all-purpose flour

2½ cups milk

2 tablespoons Dijon mustard

¼ teaspoon *each* salt and black pepper

1. Preheat oven to 400°F. Grease 13×9-inch baking dish.

2. Cut potatoes into thin slices. Layer in prepared dish; top with cheeses.

3. Melt butter in medium saucepan over medium heat. Stir in flour; cook 1 minute. Stir in milk, mustard, salt and pepper; bring to a boil. Reduce heat; cook, stirring constantly, until mixture thickens. Pour milk mixture over cheese. Cover dish with foil.

4. Bake 30 minutes. Remove foil; bake 15 to 20 minutes or until potatoes are tender and top is browned. Let stand 10 minutes.   *Makes 6 to 8 servings*

Cheesy Green Bean Casserole

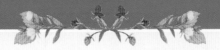

Cran-Orange Acorn Squash

3 acorn squash
5 tablespoons instant brown rice
3 tablespoons minced onion
3 tablespoons diced celery
3 tablespoons dried cranberries
  Pinch dried sage
1 teaspoon butter, cut into pieces
3 tablespoons orange juice
½ cup warm water

Slow Cooker Directions

1. Slice off tops of squash and enough of bottoms so squash will sit upright. Scoop out seeds and discard; set squash aside.

2. Combine rice, onion, celery, cranberries and sage in small bowl. Stuff each squash with rice mixture; dot with butter. Pour 1 tablespoon orange juice into each squash over stuffing. Stand squash in slow cooker. Pour water into bottom of slow cooker.

3. Cover; cook on LOW 2½ hours or until squash are tender.

Makes 6 servings

Prep Time: 20 minutes • **Cook Time:** 2½ hours

The skin of squash can defy even the sharpest knives. To make slicing easier, microwave the whole squash 5 minutes or until skin is softened.

Cran-Orange Acorn Squash

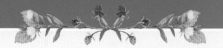

Chive & Onion Mashed Potatoes

2 pounds potatoes, peeled, quartered (about 6 cups)
½ cup milk
**1 tub (8 ounces) PHILADELPHIA® Chive & Onion Cream Cheese
  Spread**
¼ cup KRAFT® Ranch Dressing

1. Place potatoes and enough water to cover in 3-quart saucepan. Bring to
a boil.

2. Reduce heat to medium; cook 20 to 25 minutes or until tender. Drain.

3. Mash potatoes, gradually stirring in milk, cream cheese spread and dressing
until light and fluffy. Serve immediately.   *Makes 10 servings*

Prep Time: 10 minutes • **Cook Time:** 25 minutes

Make Ahead: Mix ingredients as directed; spoon into 1½-quart casserole
dish. Cover. Refrigerate several hours or overnight. When ready to serve, bake,
uncovered, at 350°F 1 hour or until heated through.

Variation: Substitute KRAFT® Three Cheese Ranch Dressing for the Ranch
Dressing.

Savory Matchstick Carrots

1 pound carrots, cut into matchstick-size pieces
½ cup water
3 tablespoons butter or margarine, cut into chunks
1½ teaspoons fresh thyme *or* ½ teaspoon dried thyme
⅛ teaspoon *each* salt and black pepper

1. Place carrots in medium saucepan; add water. Cover; bring to a boil over
high heat. Reduce heat to medium; simmer 5 to 8 minutes or until crisp-tender.

2. Drain carrots in colander. Melt butter in same saucepan over medium
heat; stir in thyme, salt and pepper. Add carrots; toss gently to coat. Serve
immediately.   *Makes 4 servings*

Chive & Onion Mashed Potatoes

Harvest Fruit Stuffing

1¾ cups **SWANSON® Chicken Broth (Regular, Natural Goodness®** or **Certified Organic)**

¼ **cup apple juice**

1 **cup cut-up mixed dried fruit**

1 **stalk celery, sliced (about** ½ **cup)**

1 **medium onion chopped (about** ½ **cup)**

5 cups **PEPPERIDGE FARM® Herb Seasoned Stuffing**

1. Stir the broth, apple juice, dried fruit, celery and onion in a large saucepan. Heat to a boil over medium-high heat. Reduce the heat to low. Cover and cook 5 minutes or until the vegetables are tender. Remove from the heat. Add the stuffing and stir lightly to coat.

2. Spoon into a 1¹/₂-quart casserole. Bake at 350°F. for 20 minutes or until hot.

Makes 8 servings

Prep Time: 20 minutes • **Cook Time:** 10 minutes • **Bake Time:** 20 minutes

Harvest Fruit Stuffing

Greens 'n' Taters

2 cups beet greens
4 potatoes, peeled and cut into 1-inch cubes
  Nonstick cooking spray
¼ cup chopped onion
1 clove garlic, minced
½ teaspoon whole fennel seeds, crushed
¼ cup plain yogurt
3 to 4 tablespoons milk
1 tablespoon butter
½ teaspoon salt
¼ teaspoon black pepper

1. Wash beet greens. Drain but do not pat dry; leave some water clinging to leaves. Remove stems; thinly slice leaves. Set aside.

2. Place potatoes and 1 inch of water in medium saucepan. Bring to a boil over high heat. Reduce heat to medium-low. Simmer, covered, 10 to 12 minutes or until potatoes are fork-tender. Drain; set aside.

3. Coat small skillet with cooking spray. Add onion, garlic and fennel seeds; cook and stir over medium heat about 5 minutes or until onion is tender. Add beet greens; cook 5 to 7 minutes or until greens are wilted and tender.

4. Mash potatoes with potato masher or beat with electric mixer; beat in yogurt, milk, butter, salt and pepper. Stir in greens mixture. Serve immediately.

Makes 6 servings

Beet tops are frequently bunched together and sold separately as beet greens. They should be fresh looking and dark green, not wilted or slimy.

Greens 'n' Taters

Pumpkin Apple Mash

2 tablespoons butter

1 small onion, chopped (about ¼ cup)

¾ cup SWANSON® Chicken Broth (Regular, Natural Goodness® or Certified Organic)

1 tablespoon packed brown sugar

¼ teaspoon dried thyme leaves, crushed

⅛ teaspoon ground black pepper

1 pumpkin or calabaza squash (about 2½ pounds), peeled, seeded and cut into 1-inch pieces (about 5 to 6 cups)

2 medium McIntosh apples, peeled, cored and cut into 1-inch pieces

1. Heat the butter in a 4-quart saucepan over medium-high heat. Add the onion and cook until the onion is tender-crisp.

2. Add the broth, brown sugar, thyme, black pepper and pumpkin and heat the mixture to a boil. Cover and reduce the heat to low. Cook for 10 minutes or until the vegetables are tender.

3. Add the apples. Cook for 5 minutes more or until the apples are tender.

4. Mash the vegetable mixture with a fork or potato masher. Serve immediately.

Makes 4 servings

Prep Time: 10 minutes • **Cook Time:** 20 minutes

Cob Corn in Barbecue Butter

4 ears fresh corn, shucked

2 tablespoons butter, softened

½ teaspoon dry barbecue seasoning

¼ teaspoon salt

1. Pour 1 inch of water into large saucepan. Bring to a boil over medium heat. Add corn; cover. Cook 4 to 6 minutes or until kernels are slightly crisp.

2. Blend butter, barbecue seasoning and salt in small bowl until smooth. Serve with corn.

Makes 4 servings

Pumpkin Apple Mash

Garlicky Mustard Greens

2 pounds mustard greens
1 teaspoon olive oil
1 cup chopped onion
2 cloves garlic, minced
¾ cup chopped red bell pepper
½ cup chicken or vegetable broth
1 tablespoon cider vinegar
1 teaspoon sugar

1. Remove stems and any wilted leaves from greens. Stack several leaves; roll up. Cut crosswise into 1-inch slices. Repeat with remaining greens.

2. Heat oil in large saucepan over medium heat. Add onion and garlic; cook and stir 5 minutes or until onion is tender. Stir in greens, bell pepper and broth. Reduce heat to low. Cook, covered, 25 minutes or until greens are tender, stirring occasionally.

3. Combine vinegar and sugar in small bowl; stir until sugar is dissolved. Stir into cooked greens; remove from heat. Serve immediately.   *Makes 4 servings*

Garlicky Mustard Greens

Sweet Endings

Deep-Dish Country Apple Pie

5 cups sliced Gala apples
3 cups sliced Granny Smith apples
1 tablespoon lemon juice
2 teaspoons vanilla
¾ cup granulated sugar
¼ cup all-purpose flour
½ teaspoon ground cinnamon
¼ teaspoon ground nutmeg
2 tablespoons butter
1 prepared refrigerated pie crust

1. Preheat oven to 425°F. Combine apples, lemon juice and vanilla in large bowl; toss to coat. Add sugar, flour, cinnamon and nutmeg; toss again. Transfer to 9-inch deep-dish pie pan. Dot with butter.

2. Cover with crust. Cut several slits in crust. Bake 50 minutes or until apples are tender. (Cover edge with foil during last 15 minutes if crust is browning too quickly.)

3. Serve warm or at room temperature. Store leftovers covered in refrigerator.

Makes 8 servings

Strawberry-Swirl Cake

1 package (2-layer size) white cake mix
1 package (4-serving size) JELL-O® Strawberry Flavor Gelatin
⅔ cup BREAKSTONE'S or KNUDSEN® Sour Cream
⅔ cup powdered sugar
1 tub (8 ounces) COOL WHIP® Whipped Topping, thawed
1 cup sliced strawberries, plus 2 whole strawberries for garnish

Preheat oven to 350°F. Grease 2 (8- or 9-inch) round cake pans; set aside. Prepare cake batter as directed on package. Pour half of the batter into medium bowl. Add dry gelatin mix; stir until well blended. Spoon half of the white batter and half of the pink batter, side by side, into each prepared pan. Lightly swirl batters together using a teaspoon. (Do not over swirl, or the color of the cake will be all pink and not pink and white marbled.)

Bake 30 minutes. Cool 30 minutes in pans. Remove to wire racks; cool completely.

Mix sour cream and powdered sugar in medium bowl until well blended. Gently stir in whipped topping. Place 1 of the cake layers on serving plate; spread top with 1 cup of the whipped topping mixture. Top with 1 cup of the strawberries and remaining cake layer. Spread top and sides of cake with remaining whipped topping mixture. Garnish with whole strawberries just before serving. Store leftover cake in refrigerator. *Makes 16 servings*

Prep Time: 35 minutes • **Total Time:** 1 hour, 35 minutes (includes cooling)

How to Prevent Air Bubbles: To release any air bubbles from the cake batter, lightly tap cake pans on counter before baking. Any small air bubbles will rise to the surface.

Strawberry-Swirl Cake

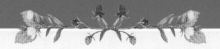

Cherry Almond Blonde Brownies

REYNOLDS® Parchment Paper
1 cup flour
1 teaspoon baking powder
¼ teaspoon salt
¾ cup packed light brown sugar
½ cup (1 stick) butter, softened
2 eggs
⅓ cup milk
1 teaspoon *each* vanilla and almond extract
¾ cup sliced almonds, coarsely chopped, divided
½ cup sweetened dried cherries
½ cup white chocolate chips

PREHEAT oven to 350°F. Line a 13×9×2-inch baking pan with Reynolds Parchment Paper, creasing folds into corners to fit pan, extending paper up sides of pan; set aside.

COMBINE flour, baking powder and salt on a sheet of parchment paper; set aside.

BEAT together brown sugar and butter in a large bowl on medium speed of an electric mixer until light and fluffy. Add eggs, milk, vanilla and almond extract; beat well. Beat in flour mixture until well blended. Stir in ½ cup almonds, cherries and white chocolate chips.

SPREAD dough evenly in parchment-lined pan. Sprinkle remaining ¼ cup almonds on top.

BAKE 25 to 27 minutes. Cool in pan on wire rack. Use edges of parchment to lift brownies from pan onto a cutting board. Pull back edges of parchment for easy cutting. Cut into bars.   *Makes 24 servings*

Prep Time: 10 minutes • **Cook Time:** 25 minutes

Cherry Almond Blonde Brownies

Apple Pecan Cheesecake

1½ cups HONEY MAID® Graham Cracker Crumbs
¼ cup (½ stick) butter, melted
2 tablespoons firmly packed brown sugar
4 packages (8 ounces each) PHILADELPHIA® Cream Cheese, softened
1½ cups firmly packed brown sugar, divided
1 teaspoon vanilla
1 cup BREAKSTONE'S® or KNUDSEN® Sour Cream
4 eggs
4 cups chopped peeled apples (about 3 medium)
¾ cup PLANTERS® Chopped Pecans
1 teaspoon ground cinnamon

1. Preheat oven to 325°F. Line 13×9-inch baking pan with foil, with ends of foil extending over sides of pan. Mix crumbs, butter and 2 tablespoons brown sugar; press firmly onto bottom of pan.

2. Beat cream cheese, 1 cup of the brown sugar and the vanilla in large bowl with electric mixer on medium speed until well blended. Add sour cream; mix well. Add eggs, 1 at a time, mixing on low speed after each addition just until blended. Pour over crust. Mix remaining ½ cup brown sugar, the apples, pecans and cinnamon; spoon evenly over cheesecake batter.

3. Bake 55 minutes or until center is almost set. Cool. Refrigerate 4 hours or overnight. Let stand at room temperature 30 minutes before serving. Lift cheesecake from pan using foil handles. Cut into 16 pieces. Store leftover cheesecake in refrigerator. *Makes 16 servings*

Prep Time: 15 minutes plus refrigerating • **Bake Time:** 55 minutes

Jazz It Up: For an extra special touch, drizzle KRAFT® Caramel Topping over each piece of cheesecake just before serving.

Best of Season: Take advantage of the many varieties of apples that are available. Try using Jonathan, Granny Smith or Honeycrisp for the topping.

Apple Pecan Cheesecake

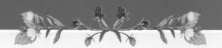

Best Fudgey Pecan Brownies

½ cup (1 stick) butter or margarine, melted
1 cup sugar
1 teaspoon vanilla extract
2 eggs
½ cup all-purpose flour
⅓ cup HERSHEY®S Cocoa
¼ teaspoon baking powder
¼ teaspoon salt
½ cup coarsely chopped pecans
Chocolate Pecan Frosting (recipe follows)
Pecan halves

1. Heat oven to 350°F. Lightly grease 8- or 9-inch square baking pan.

2. Beat butter, sugar and vanilla with spoon in large bowl. Add eggs; beat well. Stir together flour, cocoa, baking powder and salt; gradually add to egg mixture, beating until well blended. Stir in chopped pecans. Spread in prepared pan.

3. Bake 20 to 25 minutes or until brownies begin to pull away from sides of pan. Meanwhile, prepare Chocolate Pecan Frosting. Spread warm frosting over warm brownies. Garnish with pecan halves. Cool completely; cut into squares.

Makes about 16 brownies

Chocolate Pecan Frosting

1⅓ cups powdered sugar
2 tablespoons HERSHEY®S Cocoa
3 tablespoons butter or margarine
2 tablespoons milk
¼ teaspoon vanilla extract
¼ cup chopped pecans

1. Place powdered sugar and cocoa in medium bowl.

2. Heat butter and milk in small saucepan over low heat until butter is melted. Gradually beat into cocoa mixture, beating until smooth. Stir in vanilla and pecans.

Makes about 1 cup

Best Fudgey Pecan Brownies

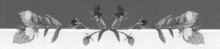

All-American Chocolate Chip Cookies

2½ cups all-purpose flour
1 teaspoon baking soda
½ teaspoon salt
1 cup (2 sticks) butter, softened
1 cup packed light brown sugar
½ cup granulated sugar
2 eggs
1 tablespoon vanilla
1 package (12 ounces) semisweet chocolate chips
1 cup coarsely chopped walnuts

1. Preheat oven to 350°F. Combine flour, baking soda and salt in medium bowl.

2. Beat butter, brown sugar and granulated sugar in large bowl with electric mixer at medium speed until light and fluffy. Beat in eggs and vanilla. Add flour mixture to butter mixture; beat until well blended. Stir in chocolate chips and walnuts, if desired.

3. Drop dough by ¼ cupfuls about 3 inches apart onto ungreased cookie sheets. Bake 12 to 14 minutes or until edges are light golden brown. Cool on cookie sheets 2 minutes. Remove to wire racks; cool completely.

Makes about 2 dozen cookies

Variation: For smaller cookies, preheat oven to 375°F. Prepare dough as directed; drop heaping teaspoonfuls onto ungreased cookie sheets. Bake 8 to 10 minutes or until edges are golden brown. Makes about 6 dozen cookies.

All-American Chocolate Chip Cookies

Perfect Pumpkin Pie

1 (15-ounce) can pumpkin (about 2 cups)
1 (14-ounce) can EAGLE BRAND® Sweetened Condensed Milk
    (NOT evaporated milk)
2 eggs
1 teaspoon ground cinnamon
½ teaspoon ground ginger
½ teaspoon ground nutmeg
½ teaspoon salt
1 (9-inch) unbaked pie crust

1. Preheat oven to 425°F.

2. In medium bowl, whisk pumpkin, EAGLE BRAND®, eggs, cinnamon, ginger, nutmeg and salt until smooth. Pour into crust.

3. Bake 15 minutes. Reduce oven temperature to 350°F and continue baking 35 to 40 minutes longer or until knife inserted 1 inch from crust comes out clean. Cool. Garnish as desired. Store leftovers covered in refrigerator.

Makes one (9-inch) pie

Prep Time: 15 minutes • **Bake Time:** 50 to 55 minutes

Sour Cream Topping: In medium bowl, combine 1½ cups sour cream, 2 tablespoons granulated sugar and 1 teaspoon vanilla extract. After pie has baked 30 minutes at 350°F, spread mixture evenly over top; bake 10 minutes longer.

Streusel Topping: In medium bowl, combine ½ cup packed brown sugar and ½ cup all-purpose flour; cut in ¼ cup (½ stick) cold butter or margarine until crumbly. Stir in ¼ cup chopped nuts. After pie has baked 30 minutes at 350°F, sprinkle streusel evenly over top; bake 10 minutes longer.

Chocolate Glaze: In small saucepan over low heat, melt ½ cup semisweet chocolate chips and 1 teaspoon solid shortening. Drizzle or spread over top of baked pie.

Perfect Pumpkin Pie

Chocolate-Raspberry Torte

1 package (8 ounces) BAKER'S® Semi-Sweet Baking Chocolate, divided
1 package (2-layer size) devil's food cake mix
1 package (8 ounces) PHILADELPHIA® Cream Cheese, softened
4 squares BAKER'S® Premium White Baking Chocolate, melted, cooled
1 tub (8 ounces) COOL WHIP® Whipped Topping, thawed, divided
1 cup seedless raspberry jam
1 cup raspberries

1. Melt 4 of the semi-sweet chocolate squares as directed on package; cool slightly. Prepare cake batter as directed on package, adding the melted semi-sweet chocolate with the water; pour into prepared 2 (9-inch) round baking pans. Bake as directed on package. Cool in pan 10 minutes; remove to wire rack. Cool completely. Wrap cake layers tightly in plastic wrap; freeze 1 hour.

2. Meanwhile, beat cream cheese in large bowl with electric mixer until creamy. Add melted white chocolate; mix well. Gently stir in half of the whipped topping. Refrigerate until ready to use.

3. Cut each cake layer horizontally in half. (You will have 4 layers.) Place 1 of the bottom cake layers on serving plate; spread top with ⅓ cup of the jam. Top with ⅔ cup of the cream cheese mixture. Repeat cake, jam and cream cheese mixture layers 2 more times; top with remaining cake layer.

4. Microwave remaining whipped topping and remaining 4 semi-sweet chocolate squares in microwaveable bowl on HIGH 1 minute; stir. Microwave an additional 30 seconds or until chocolate is melted. Stir until well blended. Spread over top of torte. Garnish with raspberries. Store in refrigerator.

Makes 18 servings

Prep Time: 25 minutes

Jazz It Up: Garnish with chocolate curls made from additional chocolate squares.

Chocolate-Raspberry Torte

Extra Chunky Peanut Butter Cookies

2 cups all-purpose flour
1 teaspoon baking soda
½ teaspoon salt
1 cup chunky peanut butter
¾ cup granulated sugar
½ cup packed light brown sugar
½ cup (1 stick) butter, softened
2 eggs
1 teaspoon vanilla
1½ cups chopped chocolate-covered peanut butter cups (12 to 14 candies)
1 cup dry roasted peanuts

1. Preheat oven to 350°F. Line cookie sheets with parchment paper or lightly grease.

2. Combine flour, baking soda and salt in medium bowl. Beat peanut butter, granulated sugar, brown sugar and butter in large bowl with electric mixer at medium speed until creamy. Beat in eggs and vanilla. Add flour mixture; beat until well blended. Stir in chopped candy and peanuts. Drop dough by rounded tablespoonfuls 2 inches apart onto prepared cookie sheets.

3. Bake 13 minutes or until set. Cool on cookie sheets 1 minute. Remove to wire racks; cool completely. *Makes about 4 dozen cookies*

To easily shape drop cookie dough into equal size cookies, use an ice cream scoop with a release bar.

Extra Chunky Peanut Butter Cookies

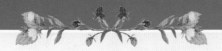

Red Velvet Cake

1 package (2-layer size) white cake mix
2 squares BAKER'S® Unsweetened Baking Chocolate, melted
1 tablespoon red food coloring
1 package (8 ounces) PHILADELPHIA® Cream Cheese, softened
½ cup (1 stick) butter or margarine, melted
1 package (16 ounces) powdered sugar (about 4 cups)
½ cup chopped PLANTERS® Pecans

1. Prepare and bake cake mix as directed on package for 2 (9-inch) round cake layers, adding chocolate and food coloring with water, eggs and oil; cool completely.

2. Beat cream cheese and butter with electric mixer on medium speed until well blended. Gradually add sugar, beating well after each addition. Stir in pecans.

3. Fill and frost cake layers with cream cheese frosting.   *Makes 16 servings*

Prep Time: 10 minutes • **Bake Time:** as directed

Contents

Cobblers & Crisps

Cinnamon Pear Crisp

  8 medium pears, peeled and sliced
  ¾ cup unsweetened apple juice concentrate
  ½ cup golden raisins
  ¼ cup plus 3 tablespoons all-purpose flour, divided
  1 teaspoon ground cinnamon
  ⅓ cup quick oats
  3 tablespoons packed dark brown sugar
  3 tablespoons butter, melted

1. Preheat oven to 375°F. Spray 11×7-inch baking dish with nonstick cooking spray.

2. Combine pears, apple juice concentrate, raisins, 3 tablespoons flour and cinnamon in large bowl; mix well. Transfer to prepared baking dish.

3. Combine oats, remaining ¼ cup flour, brown sugar and butter in medium bowl; stir until mixture resembles coarse crumbs. Sprinkle evenly over pear mixture. Bake 1 hour or until golden brown. Cool in pan on wire rack.

Makes 12 servings

Tangy Cranberry Cobbler

2 cups fresh or frozen cranberries
1 cup dried cranberries
1 cup raisins
½ cup orange juice
¼ cup plus 2 tablespoons sugar, divided
2 teaspoons cornstarch
1 cup all-purpose flour
2 teaspoons baking powder
1 teaspoon ground cinnamon
¼ teaspoon salt
¼ cup (½ stick) cold butter, cut into small pieces
½ cup milk
Vanilla ice cream or whipped cream

1. Preheat oven to 400°F. Combine cranberries, raisins, orange juice, ¼ cup sugar and cornstarch in 9-inch square baking dish; stir well.

2. Combine flour, remaining 2 tablespoons sugar, baking powder, cinnamon and salt in large bowl. Cut in butter with pastry blender or 2 knives until mixture resembles coarse crumbs. Add milk, mixing just until moistened.

3. Drop large spoonfuls of batter over cranberry mixture. Bake 35 to 40 minutes or until topping is light golden brown. Serve warm with ice cream.

Makes 6 servings

Tangy Cranberry Cobbler

Apple Toffee Crisp

5 cups (about 5 medium apples) peeled and sliced Granny Smith apples

5 cups (about 5 medium apples) peeled and sliced McIntosh apples

1¼ cups sugar, divided

1¼ cups all-purpose flour, divided

¾ cup (1½ sticks) butter or margarine, divided

1⅓ cups (8-ounce package) HEATH® BITS 'O BRICKLE® Toffee Bits

1 cup uncooked rolled oats

½ teaspoon ground cinnamon

¼ teaspoon baking powder

¼ teaspoon baking soda

¼ teaspoon salt

Whipped topping or ice cream (optional)

1. Heat oven to 375°F. Grease 13×9×2-inch baking pan.

2. Toss apple slices, ³/₄ cup sugar and ¹/₄ cup flour, coating apples evenly. Spread in bottom of prepared pan. Dot with ¹/₄ cup (¹/₂ stick) butter.

3. Stir together toffee bits, oats, remaining ¹/₂ cup sugar, remaining 1 cup flour, cinnamon, baking powder, baking soda and salt. Melt remaining ¹/₂ cup (1 stick) butter; add to oat mixture, mixing until crumbs are formed. Sprinkle crumb mixture over apples.

4. Bake 45 to 50 minutes or until topping is lightly browned and apples are tender. Serve warm with whipped topping or ice cream, if desired. Cover; refrigerate leftovers.

Makes 10 to 12 servings

Apple Toffee Crisp

Mixed Berry Crisp

6 cups mixed berries, thawed if frozen
¾ cup packed brown sugar, divided
¼ cup quick-cooking tapioca
   Juice of ½ lemon
1 teaspoon ground cinnamon
½ cup rice flour
6 tablespoons cold butter, cut into small pieces
½ cup sliced almonds

1. Preheat oven to 375°F. Grease 8- or 9-inch square baking pan.

2. Combine berries, ¼ cup brown sugar, tapioca, lemon juice and cinnamon in large bowl. Transfer to prepared pan.

3. Place rice flour, remaining ½ cup brown sugar and butter in food processor or blender. Process using on/off pulsing action until mixture resembles coarse crumbs. Add almonds; process using on/off pulsing action until combined. (Leave some large pieces of almonds.)

4. Sprinkle almond mixture over berry mixture. Bake 20 to 30 minutes or until golden brown.

Makes about 9 servings

Mixed Berry Crisp

Peach-Ginger Crumble

1 pound frozen sliced peaches, thawed
2 very ripe pears, sliced (about 6 ounces)
¾ cup dried apricots, cut into ¼-inch pieces
4 tablespoons packed dark brown sugar, divided
1 tablespoon cornstarch
1 teaspoon vanilla
12 gingersnaps
1 tablespoon canola oil
½ teaspoon ground cinnamon
Whipped cream (optional)

1. Preheat oven to 350°F. Spray 9-inch deep-dish pie plate with nonstick cooking spray.

2. Combine peaches, pears, apricots, 2 tablespoons brown sugar, cornstarch and vanilla in large bowl; toss until well blended. Transfer to prepared pie plate.

3. Place gingersnaps in large resealable food storage bag. Crush cookies with rolling pin to form coarse crumbs. Combine crumbs, remaining 2 tablespoons brown sugar, oil and cinnamon; mix well. Sprinkle evenly over peach mixture.

4. Bake 30 minutes or until fruit is bubbly. Cool 10 minutes in pan on wire rack. Top with whipped cream. *Makes 6 servings*

Peach-Ginger Crumble

Baked Apple Slices with Peanut Butter Crumble

4 cups peeled and thinly sliced apples
1 cup sugar, divided
1 cup all-purpose flour, divided
3 tablespoons butter or margarine, divided
1 cup quick-cooking or old-fashioned rolled oats
½ teaspoon ground cinnamon
1 cup REESE'S® Creamy Peanut Butter
Sweetened whipped cream or ice cream (optional)

1. Heat oven to 350°F. Grease 9-inch square baking pan.

2. Stir together apples, ¾ cup sugar and ¼ cup flour in large bowl. Spread in prepared pan; dot with 2 tablespoons butter. Combine oats, remaining ¾ cup flour, remaining ¼ cup sugar and cinnamon in medium bowl; set aside.

3. Place remaining 1 tablespoon butter and peanut butter in small microwave-safe bowl. Microwave at MEDIUM (50%) 30 seconds or until butter is melted; stir until smooth. Add to oat mixture; blend until crumbs are formed. Sprinkle crumb mixture over apples.

4. Bake 40 to 45 minutes or until apples are tender and edges are bubbly. Cool slightly. Serve warm or cool with whipped cream or ice cream, if desired.

Makes 6 to 8 servings

Baked Apple Slices with Peanut Butter Crumble

Double Cherry Crumbles

½ (18-ounce) package refrigerated oatmeal raisin cookie dough*

½ cup old-fashioned oats

¾ teaspoon ground cinnamon

½ teaspoon ground ginger

2 tablespoons cold butter, cut into small pieces

1 cup chopped pecans, toasted**

2 cans (21 ounces each) cherry pie filling

1 bag (16 ounces) frozen pitted unsweetened dark sweet cherries, thawed

*Save remaining ½ package of dough for another use.

**To toast pecans, spread in single layer on baking sheet. Bake in preheated 350°F oven 5 to 7 minutes or until golden brown, stirring frequently.

1. Let dough stand at room temperature 15 minutes. Grease 8 (½-cup) ramekins; place on baking sheet.

2. Preheat oven to 350°F. Beat dough, oats, cinnamon and ginger in large bowl until well blended. Cut in butter with pastry blender or 2 knives. Stir in pecans.

3. Combine pie filling and cherries in large bowl. Divide cherry mixture evenly among prepared ramekins; sprinkle with pecan mixture. Bake 25 minutes or until golden brown. Serve warm.   *Makes 8 servings*

Double Cherry Crumbles

Plum Cobbler with Cinnamon Drop Biscuits

6 cups sliced unpeeled ripe plums (about 12 medium)
1 cup plus 2 tablespoons all-purpose flour, divided
8 tablespoons granulated sugar, divided
¼ cup packed brown sugar
1 tablespoon lemon juice
2 teaspoons baking powder
½ teaspoon ground cinnamon
¼ teaspoon salt
¼ cup (½ stick) cold unsalted butter, cubed
8 to 10 tablespoons milk

1. Preheat oven to 400°F. Butter 8-inch square baking dish.

2. Combine plums, 2 tablespoons flour, 6 tablespoons granulated sugar, brown sugar and lemon juice in large bowl. Toss until well blended. Transfer to prepared dish. Bake 10 minutes.

3. Meanwhile, combine remaining 1 cup flour, remaining 2 tablespoons granulated sugar, baking powder, cinnamon and salt in medium bowl. Cut in butter with pastry blender or 2 knives until mixture resembles coarse crumbs. Add milk, 1 tablespoon at a time, stirring until sticky dough forms.

4. Drop heaping tablespoonfuls of dough over plum mixture. Bake 20 minutes or until golden brown. Serve warm.   *Makes 6 servings*

Plum Cobbler with Cinnamon Drop Biscuits

Peach & Berry Cobbler

Vegetable cooking spray
1 package (16 ounces) frozen peach slices
1 package (16 ounces) frozen mixed berries (strawberries, blueberries and raspberries)
1 cup V8 V-FUSION® Peach Mango juice
1 tablespoon cornstarch
1 teaspoon almond extract
1 package (18.25 ounces) yellow cake mix
1 stick butter (4 ounces), cut into pieces
Confectioners' sugar

Slow Cooker Directions

1. Spray the inside of a 6-quart slow cooker with the cooking spray. Place the peaches and berries into the cooker.

2. Stir the V8, cornstarch and almond extract in a small bowl. Pour into the cooker.

3. Sprinkle the cake mix over the fruit mixture. Dot with the butter.

4. Layer 8 pieces of paper towel across the top of the cooker. Place the cooker cover on top.*

5. Cook on LOW for 4 to 5 hours** or until the fruit mixture boils and thickens and the topping is cooked through. Sprinkle with the confectioners' sugar.

Makes 6 cups

The paper towels will absorb any moisture that rises to the top of the cooker.

**Do not lift the cover on the cooker at all during the first 3 hours of the cook time.*

Prep Time: 5 minutes • **Cook Time:** 4 to 5 hours

Peach & Berry Cobbler

Quick Breads

Fruit and Nut Loaf

¾ cup mixed dried fruit

¼ cup chopped pecans

1½ cups plus 1 tablespoon all-purpose flour, divided

½ cup whole wheat flour

¼ cup sugar

1 tablespoon baking powder

¾ teaspoon baking soda

¼ teaspoon salt

3 eggs

¾ cup orange juice

¼ cup *each* canola oil and water

1 tablespoon grated orange peel

½ teaspoon vanilla

1. Preheat oven to 350°F. Spray 8×4-inch loaf pan with nonstick cooking spray.

2. Combine fruit, pecans and 1 tablespoon all-purpose flour in small bowl; mix well. Combine remaining 1½ cups all-purpose flour, whole wheat flour, sugar, baking powder, baking soda and salt in large bowl.

3. Whisk eggs, orange juice, oil, water, orange peel and vanilla in medium bowl until well blended. Add to flour mixture; stir just until moistened. Stir in fruit mixture. Spoon into prepared pan.

4. Bake 35 to 40 minutes or until toothpick inserted into center comes out clean. Cool in pan 10 minutes. Remove to wire rack; cool completely.

Makes 12 servings

Sweet Potato Muffins

2 cups all-purpose flour
¾ cup chopped walnuts
¾ cup golden raisins
½ cup packed brown sugar
1 tablespoon baking powder
1 teaspoon ground cinnamon
½ teaspoon salt
½ teaspoon baking soda
¼ teaspoon ground nutmeg
1 cup mashed cooked sweet potato
¾ cup milk
½ cup (1 stick) butter, melted
2 eggs, beaten
1½ teaspoons vanilla

1. Preheat oven to 400°F. Grease 24 standard (2½-inch) muffin cups.

2. Combine flour, walnuts, raisins, brown sugar, baking powder, cinnamon, salt, baking soda and nutmeg in medium bowl; stir until well blended.

3. Combine sweet potato, milk, butter, eggs and vanilla in large bowl; stir until well blended. Add flour mixture to sweet potato mixture; stir just until moistened. Spoon batter evenly into prepared muffin cups.

4. Bake 15 minutes or until toothpick inserted into centers comes out clean. Cool in pans 5 minutes. Remove to wire racks; cool completely.

Makes 24 muffins

Sweet Potato Muffins

Banana Date Bread

   2 cups flour
   1½ teaspoons baking powder
   ¼ teaspoon salt
   2 eggs
   ⅔ cup KARO® Light or Dark Corn Syrup
   ½ cup MAZOLA® Oil
   1 cup mashed ripe bananas (about 2 medium)
   1 cup *each* chopped dates and chopped walnuts

1. Preheat oven to 375°F. Grease and flour 9×5×3-inch loaf pan. In medium bowl combine flour, baking powder and salt.

2. In large bowl with mixer at medium speed, beat eggs, corn syrup and oil until blended. Beat in bananas. Gradually stir in flour mixture just until moistened. Stir in dates and walnuts. Pour into prepared pan.

3. Bake 60 to 70 minutes or until toothpick inserted into center comes out clean. Cool in pan 10 minutes. Remove from pan; cool on wire rack.

Makes 1 loaf

Prep Time: 20 minutes • **Bake Time:** 70 minutes, plus cooling

Southern Biscuit Muffins

   2½ cups all-purpose flour
   ¼ cup sugar
   1½ tablespoons baking powder
   ¾ cup (1½ sticks) cold butter, cut into small pieces
   1 cup milk

1. Preheat oven to 400°F. Grease 12 standard (2½-inch) muffin cups.

2. Combine flour, sugar and baking powder in large bowl. Cut in butter with pastry blender or 2 knives until mixture resembles coarse crumbs. Add milk; stir just until moistened. Spoon evenly into prepared muffin cups.

3. Bake 20 minutes or until golden brown. Cool in pan 2 minutes. Remove to wire rack; cool completely.

Makes 12 muffins

Banana Date Bread

Maple Magic Muffins

½ cup plus 3 tablespoons maple syrup,* divided

¼ cup chopped walnuts

2 tablespoons butter, melted

2 cups all-purpose flour

¾ cup sugar

2 teaspoons baking powder

½ teaspoon baking soda

½ teaspoon salt

¼ teaspoon ground cinnamon

¾ cup plus 1 tablespoon milk

½ cup vegetable oil

1 egg

½ teaspoon vanilla

For best flavor and texture, use pure maple syrup, not pancake syrup.

1. Preheat oven to 400°F. Grease 12 standard (2½-inch) muffin cups. Place 2 teaspoons maple syrup, 1 teaspoon walnuts and ½ teaspoon butter in each muffin cup.

2. Combine flour, sugar, baking powder, baking soda, salt and cinnamon in large bowl; mix well.

3. Whisk milk, oil, egg, remaining 3 tablespoons maple syrup and vanilla in medium bowl until well blended. Add to flour mixture; stir just until blended. Spoon batter into prepared muffin cups, filling two-thirds full. Place muffin pan on baking sheet to catch any drips (maple syrup may overflow slightly).

4. Bake 20 to 25 minutes or until toothpick inserted into centers comes out clean. Invert pan onto wire rack covered with waxed paper. Cool muffins slightly; serve warm.

Makes 12 muffins

Maple Magic Muffins

Double Chocolate Zucchini Muffins

2⅓ cups all-purpose flour
1¼ cups sugar
⅓ cup unsweetened cocoa powder
2 teaspoons baking powder
1½ teaspoons ground cinnamon
1 teaspoon baking soda
½ teaspoon salt
1 cup sour cream
½ cup vegetable oil
2 eggs, beaten
¼ cup milk
1 cup milk chocolate chips
1 cup shredded zucchini

1. Preheat oven to 400°F. Line 12 jumbo (3½-inch) muffin cups with paper baking cups or spray with nonstick cooking spray.

2. Combine flour, sugar, cocoa, baking powder, cinnamon, baking soda and salt in large bowl. Combine sour cream, oil, eggs and milk in medium bowl until blended; stir into flour mixture just until moistened. Fold in chocolate chips and zucchini. Spoon batter into prepared muffin cups, filling half full.

3. Bake 25 to 30 minutes or until toothpick inserted into centers comes out clean. Cool in pans 5 minutes. Remove to wire racks; cool completely.

Makes 12 jumbo muffins

Variation: For smaller muffins, spoon batter into 18 standard (2½-inch) paper-lined or greased muffin cups. Bake at 400°F 18 to 20 minutes or until toothpick inserted into centers comes out clean.

Double Chocolate Zucchini Muffins

Apple-Cheddar Muffins

1 cup whole wheat flour
1 cup all-purpose white flour
2 tablespoons sugar
1 tablespoon baking powder
½ teaspoon salt
1 cup peeled, chopped apple
1 cup grated CABOT® Mild or Sharp Cheddar
2 large eggs
1 cup milk
4 tablespoons CABOT® Salted Butter, melted

1. Preheat oven to 400°F. Butter 12 muffin cups or coat with nonstick cooking spray.

2. In mixing bowl, stir together whole wheat and white flours, sugar, baking powder and salt. Add apples and cheese and toss to combine.

3. In another bowl, whisk eggs lightly. Whisk in milk and butter. Make well in center of dry ingredients; add milk mixture and gently stir in dry ingredients from side until just combined.

4. Divide batter among prepared muffin cups. Bake for 20 minutes, or until muffins feel firm when lightly pressed on top.   *Makes 12 muffins*

Apple-Cheddar Muffins

Ginger Squash Muffins

1½ cups all-purpose flour
⅓ cup whole wheat flour
⅓ cup granulated sugar
¼ cup packed dark brown sugar
2½ teaspoons baking powder
1 teaspoon ground cinnamon
½ teaspoon baking soda
½ teaspoon salt
½ teaspoon ground ginger
1 cup frozen winter squash, thawed*
2 eggs, beaten
⅓ cup canola oil
¼ cup finely chopped walnuts
2 tablespoons finely chopped crystallized ginger (optional)

One 12-ounce package frozen squash yields about 1 cup squash. Or, use puréed cooked fresh butternut squash.

1. Preheat oven to 375°F. Grease 12 standard (2½-inch) muffin cups.

2. Combine all-purpose flour, whole wheat flour, granulated sugar, brown sugar, baking powder, cinnamon, baking soda, salt and ground ginger in large bowl; mix well.

3. Combine squash, eggs and oil in small bowl until well blended. Add to flour mixture; stir just until blended. *Do not beat.* Stir in walnuts and crystallized ginger, if desired. Spoon batter into prepared muffin cups, filling two-thirds full.

4. Bake 18 to 20 minutes or until toothpick inserted into centers comes out clean. Cool in pan 5 minutes. Remove to wire rack; cool completely.

Makes 12 muffins

Ginger Squash Muffins

Marmalade Muffins

2 cups all-purpose flour
2 teaspoons baking powder
¾ teaspoon salt
1½ cups sugar
1 cup (2 sticks) butter, softened
2 eggs
1½ teaspoons vanilla
1 cup orange marmalade
1 cup buttermilk

1. Preheat oven to 350°F. Line 18 standard (2½-inch) muffin cups with paper baking cups.

2. Whisk flour, baking powder and salt in medium bowl.

3. Beat sugar and butter in large bowl with electric mixer at high speed 5 minutes or until light and fluffy. Add eggs, 1 at a time, beating well after each addition. Add vanilla; mix well. Fold in half of flour mixture just until moistened. Fold in marmalade and remaining flour mixture. Stir in buttermilk. *Do not overmix.* Spoon batter into prepared muffin cups, filling three-fourths full.

4. Bake 20 to 25 minutes or until toothpick inserted into centers comes out clean. Cool in pans 5 minutes. Remove to wire racks; cool completely.

Makes 18 muffins

Marmalade Muffins

Blueberry Cinnamon Muffins

1¼ cups all-purpose flour

½ cup CREAM OF WHEAT® Cinnamon Swirl Instant Hot Cereal, uncooked

½ cup sugar, divided

1 tablespoon baking powder

2 teaspoons ground cinnamon

½ teaspoon salt

1 cup fat-free milk

1 egg

2 tablespoons oil

1 teaspoon vanilla extract

1 cup fresh or frozen blueberries

2 tablespoons apple juice

1. Preheat oven to 400°F. Grease 12 standard (2½-inch) muffin cups. Mix flour, Cream of Wheat, ¼ cup sugar, baking powder, cinnamon and salt in medium bowl; set aside.

2. Beat milk, egg, oil and vanilla with wire whisk in separate bowl until well blended. Add to dry ingredients; stir just until moistened. Gently stir in blueberries. Spoon evenly into prepared muffin cups, filling each cup two-thirds full.

3. Bake 18 to 20 minutes or until toothpick inserted into centers comes out clean. Remove muffins from pan.

4. Brush tops of warm muffins with apple juice; roll in remaining ¼ cup sugar. Serve warm.

Makes 12 muffins

Prep Time: 10 minutes • **Start to Finish Time:** 30 minutes

Variation: To make Strawberries 'n Cream Muffins, use frozen strawberries and CREAM OF WHEAT® Strawberries 'n Cream Instant Hot Cereal.

Blueberry Cinnamon Muffins

Bacon-Cheddar Muffins

2 cups all-purpose flour
¾ cup sugar
2 teaspoons baking powder
½ teaspoon baking soda
½ teaspoon salt
¾ cup plus 2 tablespoons milk
⅓ cup butter, melted and cooled
1 egg
1 cup (4 ounces) shredded Cheddar cheese
6 slices bacon, crisp-cooked and crumbled

1. Preheat oven to 350°F. Grease 12 standard (2½-inch) muffin cups.

2. Combine flour, sugar, baking powder, baking soda and salt in medium bowl. Combine milk, butter and egg in small bowl; mix well. Add milk mixture to flour mixture; stir until blended. Gently stir in cheese and bacon. Spoon batter into prepared muffin cups, filling three-fourths full.

3. Bake 15 to 20 minutes or until toothpick inserted into centers comes out clean. Cool in pan 2 minutes; remove to wire rack. Serve warm or at room temperature.

Makes 12 muffins

Bacon-Cheddar Muffins

Peanut Butter Bread

¾ cup packed brown sugar
½ cup peanut butter
3 tablespoons cold butter, cut into small pieces
2 eggs
1 cup all-purpose flour
½ cup whole wheat flour
2 teaspoons baking powder
½ teaspoon ground cinnamon
¼ teaspoon salt
¼ teaspoon ground nutmeg
¼ teaspoon ground allspice
⅔ cup milk
½ teaspoon vanilla
1 cup chopped peanuts
Creamy Ginger Spread (recipe follows, optional)

1. Preheat oven to 325°F. Grease 8×4-inch loaf pan. Combine brown sugar, peanut butter and butter in food processor or blender; process until smooth. With food processor running, add eggs, 1 at a time.

2. Add all-purpose flour, whole wheat flour, baking powder, cinnamon, salt, nutmeg and allspice. Process using on/off pulsing action until well blended.

3. Pour in milk and vanilla. Process just until moistened; batter should be lumpy. *Do not overprocess.* Sprinkle peanuts over batter. Process using on/off pulsing action just until peanuts are mixed into batter. Pour batter into prepared pan.

4. Bake 1 hour or until toothpick inserted into center comes out clean. Cool in pan 15 minutes. Remove to wire rack; cool completely. Prepare Creamy Ginger Spread, if desired; serve with bread.   *Makes 12 servings*

Creamy Ginger Spread: Place 3 ounces softened cream cheese, 2 tablespoons butter, 2 tablespoons honey and ⅛ teaspoon ground ginger in food processor or blender. Process 20 to 30 seconds or until well blended. Makes about ⅔ cup.

Peanut Butter Bread

Cookies & Bars

Cobbled Fruit Bars

1½ cups apple juice
1 cup chopped dried apricots
1 cup raisins
1 package (6 ounces) dried cherries
1 teaspoon cornstarch
1 teaspoon ground cinnamon
1 package (about 18 ounces) yellow cake mix
2 cups old-fashioned oats
¾ cup (1½ sticks) butter, melted
1 egg

1. Combine apple juice, apricots, raisins, cherries, cornstarch and cinnamon in medium saucepan, stirring until cornstarch is dissolved. Bring to a boil; cook 5 minutes, stirring constantly. Remove from heat; cool to room temperature.

2. Preheat oven to 350°F. Line 15×10-inch jelly-roll pan with foil and spray lightly with nonstick cooking spray.

3. Combine cake mix and oats in large bowl; stir in butter. Add egg; stir until well blended. Press three-fourths of dough into prepared pan. Spread fruit mixture evenly over top. Sprinkle remaining dough over fruit.

4. Bake 25 to 30 minutes or until edges and top are lightly browned. Cool completely in pan on wire rack.

Makes about 1 dozen bars

Prep Time: 30 minutes • **Bake Time:** 30 minutes

Chocolate Chunk Cookies

1⅔ cups all-purpose flour

⅓ cup **CREAM OF WHEAT®** Hot Cereal (Instant, 1-minute, 2½-minute or 10-minute cook time), uncooked

½ teaspoon baking soda

¼ teaspoon salt

¾ cup (1½ sticks) butter, softened

½ cup packed brown sugar

⅓ cup granulated sugar

1 egg

1 teaspoon vanilla extract

1 (11.5-ounce) bag chocolate chunks

1 cup chopped pecans

1. Preheat oven to 375°F. Grease cookie sheets. Blend flour, Cream of Wheat, baking soda and salt in medium bowl; set aside.

2. Beat butter and sugars in large bowl with electric mixer at medium speed until creamy. Add egg and vanilla. Beat until fluffy. Reduce speed to low. Add Cream of Wheat mixture; mix well. Stir in chocolate chunks and pecans.

3. Drop by tablespoonfuls onto prepared cookie sheets. Bake 9 to 11 minutes or until golden brown. Let stand on cookie sheets 1 minute before transferring to wire racks to cool completely.

Makes 2 dozen cookies

Prep Time: 15 minutes • **Start to Finish Time:** 35 minutes

Tip: For a colorful item to take to a school bake sale or give as a gift, replace the chocolate chunks with multicolored candy-coated chocolate.

Chocolate Chunk Cookies

Gingery Oat and Molasses Cookies

1 cup all-purpose flour
¾ cup whole wheat flour
½ cup old-fashioned oats
1½ teaspoons baking powder
1½ teaspoons ground ginger
1 teaspoon baking soda
½ teaspoon ground cinnamon
¼ teaspoon salt
¾ cup sugar
½ cup (1 stick) unsalted butter, softened
1 egg
¼ cup molasses
¼ teaspoon vanilla
1 cup chopped crystallized ginger
½ cup chopped walnuts

1. Combine all-purpose flour, whole wheat flour, oats, baking powder, ground ginger, baking soda, cinnamon and salt in medium bowl.

2. Beat sugar and butter in large bowl with electric mixer at high speed until light and fluffy. Beat in egg, molasses and vanilla. Gradually beat in flour mixture. Stir in crystallized ginger and walnuts. Shape into 2 logs about 8 to 10 inches long. Wrap in plastic wrap and refrigerate 1 to 3 hours.

3. Preheat oven to 350°F. Grease cookie sheets. Cut logs into ⅓-inch slices; place 1½ inches apart on prepared cookie sheets. Bake 12 to 14 minutes or until set. Cool on cookie sheets 5 minutes. Remove to wire racks; cool completely.

Makes about 4 dozen cookies

Gingery Oat and Molasses Cookies

Carrot Cake Cookies

1½ cups all-purpose flour
1 teaspoon ground cinnamon
½ teaspoon baking soda
½ teaspoon salt
¾ cup packed brown sugar
½ cup (1 stick) butter, softened
1 egg
½ teaspoon vanilla
1 cup grated carrots (about 2 medium)
½ cup chopped walnuts
½ cup raisins or chopped dried pineapple

1. Preheat oven to 350°F. Grease cookie sheets or line with parchment paper.

2. Combine flour, cinnamon, baking soda and salt in medium bowl. Beat brown sugar and butter in large bowl with electric mixer at medium speed until creamy. Add egg and vanilla; beat until well blended. Beat in flour mixture. Stir in carrots, walnuts and raisins. Drop dough by rounded tablespoonfuls 2 inches apart onto prepared cookie sheets.

3. Bake 12 to 14 minutes or until set and edges are lightly browned. Cool on cookie sheets 1 minute. Remove to wire racks; cool completely.

Makes about 3 dozen cookies

Carrot Cake Cookies

Chocolate Seven Layer Bars

1½ cups finely crushed thin pretzels or pretzel sticks

¾ cup (1½ sticks) butter or margarine, melted

1 can (14 ounces) sweetened condensed milk (not evaporated milk)

1 package (4 ounces) HERSHEY¿S Unsweetened Chocolate Baking Bar, broken into pieces

2 cups miniature marshmallows

1 cup MOUNDS® Sweetened Coconut Flakes

1 cup coarsely chopped pecans

1 package (4 ounces) HERSHEY¿S Semi-Sweet Chocolate Baking Bar, broken into pieces

1 tablespoon shortening (do not use butter, margarine, spread or oil)

1. Heat oven to 350°F. Combine pretzels and melted butter in small bowl; press evenly onto bottom of ungreased 13×9×2-inch baking pan.

2. Place sweetened condensed milk and unsweetened chocolate in small microwave-safe bowl. Microwave at MEDIUM (50%) 1 minute; stir. If necessary, microwave at MEDIUM an additional 15 seconds at a time, stirring after each heating, until mixture is melted and smooth when stirred. Carefully pour over pretzel layer in pan. Top with marshmallows, coconut and pecans; press firmly down onto chocolate layer.

3. Bake 25 to 30 minutes or until lightly browned; cool completely in pan on wire rack.

4. Melt semi-sweet chocolate and shortening in small microwave-safe bowl at MEDIUM (50%) 1 minute or until melted when stirred; drizzle over entire top. Cut into bars. Refrigerate 15 minutes or until glaze is set.   *Makes 36 bars*

Chocolate Seven Layer Bars

Cinnamon Apple Pie Bars

1 package (about 18 ounces) spice cake mix with pudding in the mix
2 cups old-fashioned oats
½ teaspoon ground cinnamon
¾ cup (1½ sticks) cold butter, cut into pieces
1 egg
1 can (21 ounces) apple pie filling and topping

1. Preheat oven to 350°F. Spray 13×9-inch baking pan with nonstick cooking spray.

2. Combine cake mix, oats and cinnamon in large bowl. Cut in butter using pastry blender or 2 knives until butter is evenly distributed and no large pieces remain (mixture will be dry and have clumps). Stir in egg until well mixed.

3. Press about three-fourths of oat mixture evenly into bottom of prepared pan. Spread apple pie filling evenly over top. Crumble remaining oat mixture over filling.

4. Bake 25 to 30 minutes or until top and edges are lightly browned. Cool completely in pan on wire rack. Cut into bars. *Makes about 2 dozen bars*

Prep Time: 15 minutes • **Bake Time:** 30 minutes

Cinnamon Apple Pie Bars

Whoopie Pies

1 package (about 18 ounces) devil's food cake mix without pudding in the mix

1 package (4-serving size) chocolate instant pudding and pie filling mix

4 eggs

1¼ cups (2½ sticks) butter, softened, divided

1 cup water

1¼ cups marshmallow creme

¾ cup powdered sugar

½ teaspoon vanilla

1. Preheat oven to 350°F. Grease cookie sheets.

2. For cookies, beat cake mix, pudding mix, eggs, ½ cup butter and water in large bowl with electric mixer at low speed just until moistened. Beat at medium speed 2 minutes or until light and thick, scraping down side of bowl frequently. Drop batter by heaping tablespoonfuls 2 inches apart onto prepared cookie sheets.

3. Bake 12 to 14 minutes or until cookies spring back when lightly touched. Cool on cookie sheets 5 minutes. Remove to wire racks; cool completely.

4. For filling, beat remaining ¾ cup butter, marshmallow creme, powdered sugar and vanilla in large bowl at high speed 2 minutes or until light and fluffy.

5. Spread filling on flat side of half of cookies; top with remaining cookies.

Makes 2 dozen sandwich cookies

Whoopie Pies

Toffee Studded Snickerdoodles

½ cup (1 stick) butter or margarine, softened
½ cup shortening
1 cup plus 3 tablespoons sugar, divided
2 eggs
2¾ cups all-purpose flour
2 teaspoons cream of tartar
1 teaspoon baking soda
¼ teaspoon salt
1⅓ cups (8-ounce package) HEATH® BITS 'O BRICKLE® Toffee Bits
1 teaspoon ground cinnamon

1. Heat oven to 400°F.

2. Beat butter, shortening and 1 cup sugar in large bowl until fluffy. Add eggs; beat thoroughly. Stir together flour, cream of tartar, baking soda and salt; gradually add to butter mixture, beating until well blended. Stir in toffee bits.

3. Stir together remaining 3 tablespoons sugar and cinnamon. Shape dough into 1¼-inch balls; roll in sugar-cinnamon mixture. Place on ungreased cookie sheets.

4. Bake 9 to 11 minutes or until lightly browned around edges. Cool 1 minute; remove from cookie sheets to wire racks. Cool completely.

Makes about 5 dozen cookies

Toffee Studded Snickerdoodles

Extra-Chocolatey Brownie Cookies

2 cups all-purpose flour
½ cup unsweetened Dutch process cocoa powder
1 teaspoon baking soda
¾ teaspoon salt
1 cup (2 sticks) butter, softened
1 cup packed brown sugar
½ cup granulated sugar
2 eggs
2 teaspoons vanilla
1 package (11½ ounces) semisweet chocolate chunks
2 cups coarsely chopped walnuts or pecans

1. Preheat oven to 375°F. Whisk flour, cocoa, baking soda and salt in medium bowl until well blended.

2. Beat butter in large bowl with electric mixer at medium speed 1 minute or until light and fluffy. Add brown sugar and granulated sugar; beat 2 minutes or until fluffy. Add eggs and vanilla; beat until well blended. Add flour mixture; beat at low speed until blended. Stir in chocolate chunks and walnuts.

3. Drop dough by heaping tablespoonfuls 2 inches apart onto ungreased cookie sheets; flatten slightly.

4. Bake 12 minutes or until set. Cool on cookie sheets 2 minutes. Remove to wire racks; cool completely. Store in airtight container at room temperature up to 4 days.

Makes 3 dozen cookies

Prep Time: 20 minutes • **Bake Time:** 12 minutes

Extra-Chocolatey Brownie Cookies

Grandma's Favorite Sugarcakes

⅔ cup butter or margarine, softened
1½ cups packed light brown sugar
1 cup granulated sugar
2 eggs
2 teaspoons vanilla extract
4½ cups all-purpose flour
2 teaspoons baking soda
1 teaspoon baking powder
1 teaspoon salt
1 cup buttermilk or sour milk*
2 cups (12-ounce package) HERSHEY᾽S Mini Chips Semi-Sweet
    Chocolate
2 cups chopped walnuts or pecans
  Vanilla frosting (optional)
  Colored sugar or sprinkles (optional)

*To sour milk: Use 1 tablespoon white vinegar plus milk to equal 1 cup.

1. Heat oven to 350°F. Grease cookie sheet.

2. Beat butter, brown sugar and granulated sugar until well blended in large mixing bowl. Add eggs and vanilla; beat until creamy. Stir together flour, baking soda, baking powder and salt; add alternately with buttermilk to butter mixture, beating well after each addition. Stir in chocolate chips and nuts. Drop by level ¼ cups or heaping tablespoons 2 inches apart onto prepared cookie sheet.

3. Bake 12 to 14 minutes or until golden brown. Cool slightly; remove to wire rack. Cool completely. Frost with favorite vanilla frosting; garnish with colored sugar, if desired.   *Makes 3 dozen cookies*

Grandma's Favorite Sugarcakes

Lemon Drops

2 cups all-purpose flour
⅛ teaspoon salt
1 cup (2 sticks) butter, softened
1 cup powdered sugar, divided
Grated peel of 1 lemon
2 teaspoons lemon juice

1. Preheat oven to 300°F. Combine flour and salt in medium bowl.

2. Beat butter and ¾ cup powdered sugar in large bowl with electric mixer at medium speed until fluffy. Beat in lemon peel and juice until well blended. Add flour mixture, ½ cup at a time, beating just until blended after each addition.

3. Shape dough by rounded teaspoonfuls into balls. Place 1 inch apart on ungreased cookie sheets.

4. Bake 20 to 25 minutes or until lightly browned on bottom. Cool on cookie sheets 5 minutes. Remove to wire racks; cool completely. Sprinkle with remaining ¼ cup powdered sugar. *Makes about 6 dozen cookies*

Lemon Drops

Simple Cakes

Classic Angel Flake Coconut Cake

1 package (2-layer size) yellow cake mix
1 package (7 ounces) BAKER'S® ANGEL FLAKE® Coconut, divided
1 cup cold milk
1 package (4-serving size) JELL-O® Vanilla Flavor Instant Pudding
    & Pie Filling
¼ cup powdered sugar
1 tub (8 ounces) COOL WHIP® Whipped Topping, thawed

PREPARE cake batter as directed on package; stir in ⅔ cup of the coconut. Pour evenly into prepared 2 (9-inch) round baking pans. Bake as directed on package. Cool in pans 10 minutes; remove to wire racks. Cool cakes completely.

POUR milk into medium bowl. Add dry pudding mix and sugar. Beat with wire whisk 2 minutes or until well blended. (Mixture will be thick.) Gently stir in whipped topping. Refrigerate 15 minutes.

PLACE 1 cake layer on serving plate; spread top with 1 cup of the pudding mixture. Sprinkle with ¾ cup of the remaining coconut; cover with second cake layer. Spread top and side with remaining pudding mixture; press remaining coconut into pudding mixture. Refrigerate at least 1 hour. Store leftovers in refrigerator. *Makes 18 servings*

Prep Time: 25 minutes

Jazz It Up: To finish cake with toasted coconut, spread coconut in shallow baking pan. Bake in 350°F oven for 5 to 7 minutes or until browned.

Triple Chocolate Pudding Cake

1 cup biscuit baking mix
½ cup sugar
¼ cup unsweetened cocoa powder
¾ cup milk, divided
⅓ cup butter, softened
¾ cup hot fudge topping, divided
1 teaspoon vanilla
1 cup semisweet chocolate chips, divided
¾ cup coffee or hot water
Fresh raspberries (optional)

1. Preheat oven to 350°F. Grease 8-inch square baking pan.

2. Combine baking mix, sugar and cocoa in medium bowl. Beat in ½ cup milk, butter, ¼ cup hot fudge topping and vanilla until well blended. Stir in ½ cup chocolate chips. Pour batter into prepared pan.

3. Combine remaining ¼ cup milk, ½ cup hot fudge topping and coffee in small bowl; stir until well blended. Pour over batter in pan. *Do not stir.* Sprinkle remaining ½ cup chocolate chips over top.

4. Bake 45 to 50 minutes or until set. Cool in pan 15 minutes on wire rack. Spoon into dessert dishes. Garnish with raspberries. *Makes 8 servings*

Triple Chocolate Pudding Cake

Spicy Butterscotch Snack Cake

1 cup (2 sticks) butter or margarine, softened
1 cup sugar
2 eggs
½ teaspoon vanilla extract
½ cup applesauce
2½ cups all-purpose flour
1½ to 2 teaspoons ground cinnamon
1 teaspoon baking soda
½ teaspoon salt
1¾ cups (11-ounce package) HERSHEY®S Butterscotch Chips
1 cup chopped pecans (optional)
Powdered sugar or frozen whipped topping, thawed (optional)

1. Heat oven to 350°F. Lightly grease 13×9×2-inch baking pan.

2. Beat butter and sugar in large bowl until fluffy. Add eggs and vanilla; beat well. Mix in applesauce. Stir together flour, cinnamon, baking soda and salt; gradually add to butter mixture, beating until well blended. Stir in butterscotch chips and pecans, if desired. Spread in prepared pan.

3. Bake 35 to 40 minutes or until wooden pick inserted in center comes out clean. Cool completely in pan on wire rack. Dust with powdered sugar or serve with whipped topping, if desired.   *Makes 12 to 16 servings*

Spicy Butterscotch Snack Cake

Lemony Pound Cake

1 package (4-serving size) lemon-flavor gelatin
¾ cup boiling water
**1 package DUNCAN HINES® Moist Deluxe® Classic Yellow
    Cake Mix**
4 eggs
¾ cup vegetable oil
1 can (6 ounces) frozen lemonade concentrate, thawed
½ cup granulated sugar

1. Preheat oven to 350°F. Grease and flour 10-inch tube pan.

2. Dissolve gelatin in water in large mixing bowl; cool. Stir in cake mix, eggs and oil. Beat at medium speed with electric mixer for 2 minutes. Spoon into prepared pan.

3. Bake 50 minutes or until toothpick inserted in center comes out clean. Mix lemonade concentrate and sugar in small bowl. Pour over hot cake; cool in pan 1 hour. Remove from pan. Cool completely.   *Makes 12 to 16 servings*

Tip: Serve this cake with fresh or thawed frozen strawberries for a special dessert.

Lemony Pound Cake

Banana Cake

2½ cups all-purpose flour
1 tablespoon baking soda
½ teaspoon salt
1 cup granulated sugar
¾ cup packed light brown sugar
½ cup (1 stick) butter, softened
2 eggs
1 teaspoon vanilla
3 ripe bananas, mashed (about 1⅔ cups)
⅔ cup buttermilk
1 container (16 ounces) dark chocolate frosting

1. Preheat oven to 350°F. Grease two 8-inch round cake pans. Combine flour, baking soda and salt in medium bowl.

2. Beat granulated sugar, brown sugar and butter in large bowl with electric mixer at medium speed until well blended. Add eggs and vanilla; beat well. Stir in bananas. Alternately add flour mixture and buttermilk; beat until well blended after each addition. Pour batter into prepared pans.

3. Bake 35 minutes or until toothpick inserted into centers comes out clean. Cool in pans 10 minutes. Remove to wire racks; cool completely.

4. Fill and frost cake with chocolate frosting.   *Makes 12 to 16 servings*

Banana Cake

Apple Spice Custard Cake

1 (18.25-ounce) package spice cake mix
2 medium apples, peeled, cored and chopped
1 (14-ounce) can EAGLE BRAND® Sweetened Condensed Milk
  (NOT evaporated milk)
1 (8-ounce) container sour cream
¼ cup lemon juice
  Ground cinnamon (optional)

1. Preheat oven to 350°F. Grease and flour 13×9-inch baking pan.

2. Prepare cake mix according to package directions. Stir in apples. Pour batter into prepared pan. Bake 30 to 35 minutes or until toothpick inserted near center comes out clean.

3. In medium bowl, combine EAGLE BRAND® and sour cream; mix well. Stir in lemon juice. Remove cake from oven; spread sour cream mixture evenly over hot cake.

4. Return to oven; bake 5 minutes or until set. Sprinkle with cinnamon (optional). Cool. Chill. Store leftovers covered in refrigerator.

Makes one (13×9-inch) cake

Prep Time: 15 minutes • **Bake Time:** 35 to 40 minutes

Apple Spice Custard Cake

Rocky Road Cake

1 cup chopped walnuts or pecans
1 package (about 18 ounces) devil's food cake mix
1⅓ cups water
3 eggs
½ cup vegetable oil
2 teaspoons instant coffee granules (optional)
4 cups miniature marshmallows
1 container (16 ounces) hot fudge topping

1. Preheat oven to 350°F. Grease 13×9-inch baking pan.

2. Toast walnuts in medium skillet over medium-high heat 5 minutes or just until beginning to brown, stirring frequently. Remove from heat; cool completely.

3. Beat cake mix, water, eggs, oil and coffee granules, if desired, in large bowl with electric mixer at low speed 1 minute or until well blended. Pour into prepared pan.

4. Bake 33 minutes or until toothpick inserted into center comes out almost clean. Immediately sprinkle marshmallows evenly over cake; top with walnuts. Let stand on wire rack 15 minutes.

5. Heat hot fudge topping in microwave according to package directions. Drizzle evenly over cake. Cool completely.

Makes 16 servings

Rocky Road Cake

Pineapple Upside-Down Cake

Topping

½ cup (1 stick) butter or margarine

1 cup firmly packed brown sugar

1 can (20 ounces) pineapple slices, well drained

Maraschino cherries, drained and halved

Walnut halves

Cake

1 package DUNCAN HINES® Moist Deluxe® Pineapple Supreme Cake Mix

1 package (4-serving size) vanilla-flavor instant pudding and pie filling mix

4 eggs

1 cup water

½ cup oil

1. Preheat oven to 350°F.

2. For topping, melt butter over low heat in 12-inch cast-iron skillet or skillet with ovenproof handle. Remove from heat. Stir in brown sugar. Spread to cover bottom of skillet. Arrange pineapple slices, maraschino cherries and walnut halves in skillet. Set aside.

3. For cake, combine cake mix, pudding mix, eggs, water and oil in large mixing bowl. Beat at medium speed with electric mixer for 2 minutes. Pour batter evenly over fruit in skillet. Bake at 350°F for 1 hour or until toothpick inserted into center comes out clean. Invert onto serving plate.

Makes 16 to 20 servings

Variation: Cake can be made in a 13×9×2-inch pan. Bake at 350°F for 45 to 55 minutes or until toothpick inserted into center comes out clean. Cake is also delicious using Duncan Hines® Moist Deluxe® Classic Yellow Cake Mix.

Pineapple Upside-Down Cake

Sweet and Sour Brunch Cake

1 package (16 ounces) frozen rhubarb, thawed and patted dry

1 cup packed brown sugar

1 tablespoon all-purpose flour

1 teaspoon ground cinnamon

¼ cup (½ stick) cold butter, cut into small pieces

1 package (about 18 ounces) yellow cake mix without pudding in the mix

1 package (4-serving size) vanilla instant pudding and pie filling mix

4 eggs

⅔ cup sour cream

½ cup water

½ cup vegetable oil

1. Preheat oven to 350°F. Spray 13×9-inch baking pan with nonstick cooking spray.

2. Spread rhubarb evenly in single layer in prepared pan. Combine brown sugar, flour and cinnamon in small bowl; mix well. Sprinkle evenly over rhubarb; dot with butter.

3. Beat cake mix, pudding mix, eggs, sour cream, water and oil in large bowl with electric mixer at low speed 1 minute. Beat at medium speed 2 minutes or until well blended. Pour batter into prepared pan, spreading carefully over rhubarb mixture.

4. Bake 40 to 50 minutes or until toothpick inserted into center comes out clean. Cool in pan 5 minutes; invert onto serving platter.

Makes 16 to 18 servings

Note: If frozen rhubarb is unavailable, substitute frozen unsweetened strawberries.

Sweet and Sour Brunch Cake

Best Ever Chocolate Fudge Layer Cake

1 package (2-layer size) chocolate cake mix

1 package (4-serving size) JELL-O® Chocolate Flavor Instant
    Pudding & Pie Filling

4 eggs

1 cup BREAKSTONE'S® or KNUDSEN® Sour Cream

½ cup vegetable oil

½ cup water

1 package (8 squares) BAKER'S® Semi-Sweet Baking Chocolate,
    divided

1 tub (8 ounces) COOL WHIP® Whipped Topping, thawed

2 tablespoons PLANTERS® Sliced Almonds

PREHEAT oven to 350°F. Lightly grease 2 (9-inch) round cake pans. Beat cake mix, dry pudding mix, eggs, sour cream, oil and water in large bowl with electric mixer on low speed just until moistened, scraping side of bowl frequently. Beat on medium speed 2 minutes or until well blended. Stir in 2 squares of the chocolate, chopped. Spoon into prepared pans.

BAKE 30 to 35 minutes or until toothpick inserted near centers comes out clean. Cool in pans 10 minutes on wire rack. Loosen cakes from side of pans with spatula or knife. Invert cakes onto rack; gently remove pans. Cool completely on wire rack.

PLACE remaining 6 squares chocolate and whipped topping in medium microwaveable bowl. Microwave on HIGH 1½ to 2 minutes. Stir until well blended and shiny. Cool 5 minutes. Place 1 cake layer on serving plate; spread ¼ of the chocolate mixture over cake. Place second cake layer on top; spread remaining chocolate mixture over top and sides of cake. Garnish with almonds.

Makes 18 servings

Prep Time: 10 minutes • **Total Time:** 1 hour, 10 minutes

Best Ever Chocolate Fudge Layer Cake

Favorite Potluck Carrot Cake

1 package (about 18 ounces) yellow cake mix
1 package (4-serving size) vanilla instant pudding and pie filling
    mix
3 cups grated carrots
1 can (8 ounces) crushed pineapple, undrained
4 eggs
½ cup chopped walnuts
½ cup water
2 teaspoons ground cinnamon
2 packages (8 ounces each) cream cheese, softened
½ cup (1 stick) butter, softened
2 teaspoons vanilla
2 cups powdered sugar, sifted

1. Preheat oven to 350°F. Spray 13×9-inch baking dish with nonstick cooking spray.

2. Combine cake mix, pudding mix, carrots, pineapple, eggs, walnuts, water and cinnamon in large bowl. Beat with electric mixer at low speed 30 seconds. Beat at medium speed 2 minutes. Pour batter into prepared dish.

3. Bake 40 to 45 minutes or until toothpick inserted into center comes out clean. Cool completely in dish on wire rack.

4. Beat cream cheese, butter and vanilla in medium bowl with electric mixer at medium-high speed 2 minutes or until fluffy. Gradually add powdered sugar, beating well after each addition. Spread over top of cake.

Makes 12 to 15 servings

Favorite Potluck Carrot Cake

Chocolate-Peanut Butter Cake

What You Need

    1 package (2-layer size) devil's food cake mix

    1 package (8 ounces) PHILADELPHIA® Cream Cheese, softened

    ¾ cup powdered sugar

    ½ cup peanut butter

    1 tub (8 ounces) COOL WHIP® Whipped Topping, thawed, divided

    6 squares BAKER'S® Semi-Sweet Chocolate

Make It

PREPARE cake batter and bake in 13×9-inch pan as directed on package; cool completely.

BEAT cream cheese and sugar in large bowl with mixer on medium-low speed until well blended. Add peanut butter; mix well. Blend in 1 cup COOL WHIP®; spread onto cake.

PLACE chocolate in medium microwaveable bowl. Microwave on HIGH 2 minutes or until completely melted, stirring with whisk after each minute. Stir in remaining 2 cups COOL WHIP®; spread over cake. Refrigerate until set. Store in refrigerator. *Makes 24 servings*

Prep Time: 20 minutes

Chocolate-Peanut Butter Cake

Upside-Down Peach Corn Bread Cakes

¼ cup (½ stick) butter
½ cup packed light brown sugar
1 fresh peach, thinly sliced
2 packages (8½ ounces each) corn bread mix
2 eggs
½ cup milk
2 tablespoons vegetable oil
1¾ cups diced fresh peaches or frozen diced unsweetened peaches, thawed

1. Preheat oven to 400°F. Spray 8 standard (2½-inch) muffin cups or ramekins with nonstick cooking spray. Place 1½ teaspoons butter and 1 tablespoon brown sugar in bottom of each muffin cup. Divide peach slices equally among muffin cups.

2. Whisk together corn bread mix, eggs, milk and oil in large bowl. Stir in diced peaches. Pour ¾ cup batter into each muffin cup.

3. Bake 20 minutes or until golden and toothpick inserted into centers comes out clean. Let cool 5 minutes. Run knife around edges; invert cakes onto serving plates.

Makes 8 servings

Serving Suggestion: Serve with whipped cream or a scoop of vanilla ice cream, if desired.

Acknowledgments

The publisher would like to thank the companies and organizations listed below for the use of their recipes and photographs in this publication.

ACH Food Companies, Inc.

The Beef Checkoff

Cabot® Creamery Cooperative

Campbell Soup Company

ConAgra Foods, Inc.

Cream of Wheat® Cereal

Duncan Hines® and Moist Deluxe® are registered trademarks of Pinnacle Foods Corp.

EAGLE BRAND®

The Hershey Company

Hillshire Farm®

Hormel Foods, LLC

Idaho Potato Commission

Jennie-O Turkey Store, LLC

©2010 Kraft Foods, KRAFT, KRAFT Hexagon Logo, PHILADELPHIA AND PHILADELPHIA Logo are registered trademarks of Kraft Foods Holdings, Inc. All rights reserved.

Minnesota Cultivated Wild Rice Council

National Onion Association

National Turkey Federation

Newman's Own, Inc.®

North Dakota Wheat Commission

Ortega®, A Division of B&G Foods, Inc.

Reckitt Benckiser Inc.

Recipes courtesy of the Reynolds Kitchens

Tyson Foods, Inc.

Index

Metric Conversion Chart

VOLUME MEASUREMENTS (dry)

¹/₈ teaspoon = 0.5 mL
¹/₄ teaspoon = 1 mL
¹/₂ teaspoon = 2 mL
³/₄ teaspoon = 4 mL
1 teaspoon = 5 mL
1 tablespoon = 15 mL
2 tablespoons = 30 mL
¹/₄ cup = 60 mL
¹/₃ cup = 75 mL
¹/₂ cup = 125 mL
²/₃ cup = 150 mL
³/₄ cup = 175 mL
1 cup = 250 mL
2 cups = 1 pint = 500 mL
3 cups = 750 mL
4 cups = 1 quart = 1 L

VOLUME MEASUREMENTS (fluid)

1 fluid ounce (2 tablespoons) = 30 mL
4 fluid ounces (¹/₂ cup) = 125 mL
8 fluid ounces (1 cup) = 250 mL
12 fluid ounces (1¹/₂ cups) = 375 mL
16 fluid ounces (2 cups) = 500 mL

WEIGHTS (mass)

¹/₂ ounce = 15 g
1 ounce = 30 g
3 ounces = 90 g
4 ounces = 120 g
8 ounces = 225 g
10 ounces = 285 g
12 ounces = 360 g
16 ounces = 1 pound = 450 g

DIMENSIONS

¹/₁₆ inch = 2 mm
¹/₈ inch = 3 mm
¹/₄ inch = 6 mm
¹/₂ inch = 1.5 cm
³/₄ inch = 2 cm
1 inch = 2.5 cm

OVEN TEMPERATURES

250°F = 120°C
275°F = 140°C
300°F = 150°C
325°F = 160°C
350°F = 180°C
375°F = 190°C
400°F = 200°C
425°F = 220°C
450°F = 230°C

BAKING PAN SIZES

Utensil	Size in Inches/Quarts	Metric Volume	Size in Centimeters
Baking or Cake Pan (square or rectangular)	8×8×2	2 L	20×20×5
	9×9×2	2.5 L	23×23×5
	12×8×2	3 L	30×20×5
	13×9×2	3.5 L	33×23×5
Loaf Pan	8×4×3	1.5 L	20×10×7
	9×5×3	2 L	23×13×7
Round Layer Cake Pan	8×1½	1.2 L	20×4
	9×1½	1.5 L	23×4
Pie Plate	8×1¼	750 mL	20×3
	9×1¼	1 L	23×3
Baking Dish or Casserole	1 quart	1 L	—
	1½ quart	1.5 L	—
	2 quart	2 L	—